# INDEPENDENT LEARNING

## in the Foundation Stage

*Sally Featherstone and Ros Bayley*

Published 2011 by A&C Black Publishers Limited
36 Soho Square, London W1D 3QY
www.acblack.com

ISBN 978-1-4081-406-66

First published in the UK in 2002 by Featherstone Education as
Foundations for Independence

Text © Ros Bayley, Sally Featherstone 2002
Photographs © Sam Goodman 2011
Design by Bob Vickers

Cover photographs © Shutterstock

A CIP record for this publication is available from the British Library.

Printed in Great Britain by Latimer Trend & Company Limited

This book is produced using paper that is made from wood grown
in managed, sustainable forests. It is natural, renewable and recyclable.
The logging and manufacturing processes conform to the environmental
regulations of the country of origin.

**To see our full range of titles
visit www.acblack.com**

# Contents

# Introduction

This book is for everyone working in, or with an interest in early childhood education. We hope that it will provoke discussions about the nature of early learning, and offer help in recognising success and planning for change in response to the interests of the children and their learning.

*Independent Learning in the Foundation Stage* is divided into four sections and eighteen chapters.

## Section 1: Setting the Scene

Chapter 1 introduces the notion of independence in young children and establishes the context for what follows. Chapter 2 looks at the development of views of the education of young children. It traces the theories which dominate present-day approaches, locating the sources of our continuing emphasis on play, first hand experiences, the outdoor curriculum, socialisation, language and working together. Chapter 3 reviews recent research into how the brain develops and relates this to the education of young children. It also explores contemporary pressures on early years practitioners and settings, and suggests ways of responding to them.

## Section 2: Developing Independent Learners

Chapter 4 defines independence, what it is and how it develops, and discusses the essential skills and attributes which support independent learning. Chapter 5 looks at the role of adults in promoting and supporting independent learning, and Chapter 6 examines the influence of the setting and the environment, and describes the conditions children need to become independent learners.

## Section 3: Promoting Independent Learning

This section is intended mainly for practitioners and managers. It takes key features of the early years curriculum, relates them to Early Learning Goals and, with the help of case studies, gives advice and guidance on providing them in settings.

## Section 4: Managing the Learning

Chapter 8 describes two important and influential approaches to the early years, that of the schools in Reggio Emilia and the High/Scope programme.

It describes both approaches in action and examines how and why they are so successful in developing independence in children. It identifies common features and suggests what can be learned and adapted to UK settings. Chapter 9 explores some of the issues for managers in promoting independence as a principle of their setting, and discusses involving parents and those outside the setting in developing this independence.

The Bibliography lists most of the works we have used and relied on in writing this book. At the end we provide a quality checklist, Ten Essential Elements of a Successful Early Years Foundation Stage. Throughout the book you will find quotations from other works, which support and amplify our approach to independent learning, and sometimes offer examples, illustrations or further information.

A highly illustrated companion volume, *Child-Initiated Learning* (A & C Black), which supports the practical ideas in Section 3, is also available.

Sally Featherstone and Ros Bayley; November 2010

# Section 1

# Setting the Scene

# Chapter 1:
# Recognising independent learning

The independence of the individual is at the heart of a free and democratic society. The capacity to become involved in one's own learning, to take responsibility for it, and to manage it are keys to success in school and beyond. So the independent learner is sought, not only by teachers and parents, but by employers and in society at large. What is not so universally agreed is the precise nature of independent learning and the skills needed for it.

> Research reveals that schools and employers have quite different priorities. Skills which are regarded as 'softer skills' by schools are considered by employers to be far more valuable than the three main key skills (IT, communication and the application of number). Employers listed leadership, organisational skills, confidence and the ability to negotiate as key to success at work. Employers were concerned that school leavers lacked initiative and often had unrealistic ideas about work and poor social skills.
>
> *TES 25/05/01*

What, then, is an independent learner? What are the skills needed for independent learning? Why are they important, and how do we encourage their development in an education system, which in the recent past, has emphasised content and cognitive ability, with vital skills for learning following in a very slow second place?

> ...the key ingredient in independent learning was the shift of responsibility for the learning process from the teacher to the pupil.
>
> *What is independent learning and what are the benefits for pupils? (A literature review of Independent Learning; Bill Meyer, Naomi Haywood, Darshan Sachdev and Sally Faraday; Department for Children, Schools and Families Research Report 051, 2008)*

Each of the four constituent countries of the UK has introduced a national framework for the development of key learning skills from three to 18. At the heart of each of these is an acknowledgement of the importance of cross-curricular key skills, including the central driver for success - the independent learner.

For the most part, when teachers talk about children, they inevitably

*Independent Learning in the Foundation Stage*

talk about individuals, with skills, attributes and attitudes to learning. However, discussion among professionals who work with children won't go on for long before referring to the weight of a multitude of content-laden initiatives, the heavy burden of paperwork and the pressures of increased accountability in performance management, target setting and inspection, all of which can easily focus on 'measuring the easily measurable'. Any programme for developing the skills of individuals will have to compete with such pressures, now extended to settings for children from soon after birth.

## Three different types of behaviour

We believe that encouraging and enabling children from an early age to think for themselves, take responsibility for what they do and play a major part in managing their own learning is vital if they are to be successful adults, workers and citizens in the 21st century. To illustrate our point, here are three short studies of children in early years settings. They are all based on real people that we knew well. No doubt readers will recognise some of these characteristics in children they know.

### DALBIR

Dalbir walks with great purpose towards her nursery. She urges her mother to walk more quickly. Over breakfast she has been busy talking to her mum about what she intends to do at nursery, and is extremely clear about how she wants to spend her time.

Her mother quickens her pace, conscious that Dalbir is anxious to share her plans with her best friend Adam, and enthuse him with the idea of building a house in the large construction area.

As soon as they arrive at the setting, Dalbir finds her name card and hangs it on the board to register her arrival. She spots Adam coming through the door and hurries to find his name card for him. As she hands it to him she talks excitedly about her ideas for building a house and they begin to share their plans for the morning. Dalbir listens carefully to what Adam has to say. She realises that he has come to school bearing a selection of boxes which he wants to use to make a model of a dinosaur.

She makes a suggestion. 'I've got an idea,' she says, 'I'll help you with your model and then we could build a house!'

'That would be good,' replies Adam. 'The dinosaur can guard the house! I'll put the newspaper on the table and you get the glue and some tape.'

There is no hesitation. Dalbir and Adam begin to make preparations for their joint project. They proceed to work with concentration and perseverance, seeking assistance from the adults in the room only when they have

repeated difficulty in joining one part of the dinosaur to another. On completion of the model making they carefully carry the dinosaur to the painting area, where they cover it with green and purple paint.

'He can't guard the house 'til he's dry,' declares Adam, who is writing his own and Dalbir's name on a white sticky label. As Adam proudly sticks the label on the model, Dalbir suggests that they should come back for the dinosaur when the house is ready. They hurry away to the large construction area.

## GEORGE

George stands in the cloakroom beside his peg, waiting patiently as his mother unbuttons his coat and hangs it up. He seems reluctant to say goodbye to her but eventually he gives her a kiss and lets her go. He stands by the window, waving until she is out of sight.

Mandy, his key person, conscious that he has not yet joined the group, calls him over to sit on the carpet with the other children but George appears not to hear her. Lost in his own thoughts he stays rooted to the spot. Mandy leaves the group, and taking him by the hand brings him over to sit on the carpet for registration.

Once the register is marked the children take their places at tables ready for a focused teaching session. The adults explain the task and give out materials. Some of the children get started but George sits quietly at the art table, showing little interest in any of the materials. Mandy asks him what he would like to paint, but he says he doesn't know. She makes several suggestions but George doesn't respond to any of them. Eventually he picks up the paintbrush and tentatively makes some marks on his paper.

He seems happy to do this and continues until most of the paper is covered. He puts down his brush and waits patiently until an adult helper writes his name in a corner of the paper and helps him take his painting to the drying rack. As they are doing this, another child, rushing to put her painting to dry, trips over and bumps into George, spreading paint on his sweatshirt. George doesn't say anything, he just bursts into a flood of tears. Mandy tells him that they can easily sponge the paint from his sweatshirt. She urges him to take it off but George makes no response. He continues to stand still, crying with renewed vigour. Not wanting him to be further distressed, she peels off his sweatshirt and wipes his eyes with a tissue. In no time at all, his sweatshirt is returned with the paint removed and an adult helper puts it back on for him.

The children are now given access to a wide range of activities and, while most of them are keen to get started, George stays close to his base. Eventually he picks up a car and begins to push it backwards and forwards over the playmat. He continues to do this until it is snack time.

*Independent Learning in the Foundation Stage*

## KEVIN

Kevin runs into his reception class. He is pretending to be an aeroplane! His teacher asks him to sit down with the rest of the children. Kevin ignores her request and continues to hurtle around the carpet area, bumping into children as he goes. Anxious that the other children should not be hurt, his teacher repeats her request more firmly. Kevin complies, and sits on the carpet.

As soon as everyone is settled and the register has been called, they begin a shared reading session. The children join in, really enjoying the story of 'Mrs Wishy Washy,' although Kevin's attempts to dominate the proceedings detract from the other children's pleasure. He persistently stands up, waves his arms and shouts out, demanding a great deal of the practitioner's attention.

Following this session, the children are told which groups will do what. While some of the children continue to work with adults on adult-initiated activities, others are engaged in child-initiated activities, supported by another practitioner. Kevin, who is in this second group, hurtles off towards the sand tray and begins furiously digging in the sand. After only a few moments he has scraped all the sand and most of the toys to one end of the sand tray. The other children at the sand tray have nothing to play with.

'We need some sand too,' says Rosie, as she begins to drag some of the sand back with her cupped hands.

'Get off,' shouts Kevin. 'I need all of it!'

'That's not fair,' persists Rosie, snatching back some of the toys.

Kevin grabs the other end of the sand rake and begins to tug at it. 'GIVE IT ME!' he shouts, but Rosie is not to be beaten. She pulls and twists until she finally manages to wrench the rake from Kevin's hands. Kevin, angered by his defeat, throws handfuls of sand into Rosie's face. With her eyes, hair and mouth full of sand, Rosie begins to howl loudly. An adult hurries over to intervene.

There is probably not much doubt which of these behaviours most practitioners would prefer to see in the children in their groups, or which of these children would be the most rewarding to teach. But what is it that accounts for these three very different attitudes? The home? The setting? Different personalities? You may like to ask yourself these questions:

- What do Dalbir, George and Kevin tell us about the emergence of independence in young children?
- What is the difference between independence and self will? Are they both equally desirable?

- Which of the three children is likely to be the most successful long-term learner, and to make best use of the opportunities of school and adult life?
- Is it at all significant that Dalbir is female and the other two children are male?
- What are the essential skills and attributes that support independent learning?
- Is it nature, nurture or something else that enables children to manage their own learning?
- Is independence something we can influence, something we can identify and provide for?
- How does independence develop? What are the key stages in its development, and what can parents, practitioners and other adults do at the early stages of learning to help children to become more independent?
- Where does independence flourish? What is the best environment for its development?
- Are there particular schools or school programmes where independence is encouraged and children demonstrate all the skills we value?

We shall return to these questions throughout this book, and try to suggest some answers. Our work in researching and writing has led us to revisit and incorporate the thoughts of some of the people who have most influenced practice in early years education:

> **specialists** (theoreticians, philosophers, child psychologists, researchers, policy makers and practitioners from the 17th century to the present day, including those who enquire into how the human brain works and develops)
>
> **current practitioners** in internationally recognised schools and systems where the principles of independent learning are valued and promoted.

We have also drawn on the thoughts, practice and experience of a huge number of practitioners in the many settings we have been privileged to visit and work with as teachers, consultants and trainers.

In the best practice we have seen, the promotion and development of independence in the Foundation Stage has been a key feature of the practitioner's work. All of them agree that the most valuable tools we can give to children are the abilities to choose, to think for themselves, to negotiate, to work collaboratively, to question, reflect, find out, concentrate and persevere. These are also the abilities which will give children a sound basis for lifelong learning.

*Independent Learning in the Foundation Stage*

The capacity to think and act independently, to assume control of and responsibility for one's own behaviour, requires support and good models, particularly from the adults who are closest to the children. We have identified, both in our research and in this book, elements of good practice in adult roles and interactions with children. We have also included some guidance on involving parents in the discussion of the characteristics of independent learners.

The environment in which children learn is a potent force for helping them develop their independence. We have selected a range of activities and for each we have suggested what can be done to help children manage their own work and learning. We have also linked each with the relevant parts of the Guidance for the early years in England, across the UK and throughout the world.

> Children are strong, rich and capable. All children have preparedness, potential, curiosity and interest in constructing their learning, negotiating with everything their environment brings to them.
>
> *Lella Gandini, Reggio Emilia*

Chiefly, however, it is the children themselves whose enthusiasm, energy, wonder and spirit of enquiry must be harnessed and guided in directions that enable them to flex and then confidently fly on the wings of independence. Harnessed and guided, not directed. As John Holt has written:

> Children are born passionately eager to make as much sense as they can of things around them. The process by which children turn experience into knowledge is exactly the same, point for point, as the process by which those we call scientists make scientific knowledge. Children observe, they wonder, they speculate, and they ask themselves questions. They think up possible answers, they make theories, they hypothesise, and then they test theories by asking questions or by further observations or experiments or reading. Then they modify the theories as needed or reject them and the process continues. If we attempt to control, manipulate, or divert this process, we disturb it. If we continue this long enough, the process stops. The independent scientist in the child disappears.
>
> *John Holt, Learning All The Time; DeCapo Press; 1990*

Supporting the 'emerging scientist' is hard work. It is a sensitive, thoughtful activity, involving us in observation, listening, open questioning, taking risks and trusting judgement. Independence does not come cheap, in any sense. It requires patience, dedication, good planning and preparation and a high quality environment. It also takes strength of mind and purpose if the pressures and prescriptions that society sometimes forces on educators are to be managed in the best interests of the children with whom we work.

# Chapter 2:
# The story of pre-five education and the child as independent thinker

It has been said that those who know no history are condemned to relive it. It therefore seemed sensible in planning this book to start by looking at how we got to where we are today. What are the factors, and particularly who are the thinkers, that have contributed to the context in which we work? And what have some of these thinkers concluded about the questions we posed in the last chapter: is it nature, nurture or something else that enables children to manage their own learning? Where has the emphasis on independence come from? Is it new?

Our visit to some of these great minds is necessarily cursory and brief, and because of this we make generalisations and simplifications. Those who wish to go deeper and to find out more are encouraged to go directly to the works we used.

## In the beginning

Until comparatively recently children were viewed as miniature adults. As such they possessed most of an adult's characteristics and joined in adult activities. For the lower social classes there was an expectation that children would work, and virtually every family in these groups depended on the contribution of children to the family income. Children had no innocence that needed to be protected. As soon as they were weaned they ate, drank and dressed like adults. They worked alongside their parents, and play was considered a pointless activity, something from which children should be discouraged.

Around the turn of the 18th century a view began to grow that childhood was a stage in its own right: not just a preparation for adulthood but a phase of human development that had a place and a purpose all of its own. Those involved in observing the ways in which children learn became

> Sturdy carts, small gardening tools, printing presses, looms and furniture which takes to pieces and reassemble ...
> pencils, scissors, paste, tools and workbenches.
>
> *Maria Edgeworth setting out in 1789 the requirements for educating a young learner.*

fascinated by the place of play in helping thinking, learning and independence.

A landmark in the emergence of this new view of childhood was the work of the French philosopher, Jean Jacques Rousseau. Rousseau's controversial book on upbringing, *Emile*, was written in 1762. It placed a high value on the freedom of action of the child by promoting 'self or free activity' in an education rooted in the natural world. In Emile's education there were no books, no schools, and all lessons were based on direct experience of and interaction with the outside world. Emile learnt by doing, with the help of supportive adults. This philosophy, which has been described as emphasising 'the personal experience of the child, supported by loving encouragement' will be familiar to readers as not being too far removed from what is generally considered good practice today. Its principles were:

- that childhood is a sacred period
- that a child's first hand explorations are the engine of the expanding mind
- that education should be provided through action, with direct and first hand observation
- that adults should provide support and guidance rather than the mere teaching of facts.

These views were radical when first written and they aroused much opposition. Today many subscribe to their essence and spirit. We may not realise it, but the principles Rousseau set out in *Emile* still affect the way we work with children. The child-centred approach he promoted forms the foundation of the modern approach to education in the early years. P.D.Jimack, in his introduction to *Emile*, rightly points out that '...many of Rousseau's principles, in particular on the psychology of learning, anticipate uncannily the findings of modern scientific investigators.'

*Emile* was criticised by many but the work had a profound influence on the future of both child rearing and education across the world. It was taken up and built upon by the great educational thinkers of the late 18th and early 19th centuries. For example, Pestalozzi promoted the essential foundation of learning within the home in a loving relationship with parents. He established schools promoting 'natural' education, 'where the innate desire to learn is nourished and curiosity is unfettered.' These schools were

> A child's explorations are the engine of the expanding mind. It matters little what he learns, provided he understands it and knows how to use it.
>
> *Jean Jacques Rousseau, Emile;*
> *Phoenix; 1993*

characterised by their commitment to hands-on experiences and direct observation, natural equality and personal freedom. The children who attended them were not exclusively the children of the upper or middle classes. Pestalozzi's first school in Switzerland opened its doors to orphans and the children of peasants and helped to promote the principle of education as a right for all.

> Our first teachers of philosophy are our feet, our hands and our eyes.
>
> *Pestalozzi*

One of Rousseau's most ardent admirers and eminent followers was Friedrich Froebel. Froebel also believed in the importance of an early start to education. He gave precise advice to parents in a seminal book for mothers of children from four months old, *Mother Play and Nursery Songs*. Froebel's philosophy and methods were explored and expanded in the kindergarten movement of which he was the founder and which became a worldwide influence, spreading from Germany to Scandinavia and the rest of Northern Europe, the USA, the Far East and beyond.

Froebel's emphasis on practical experience and play embraced the views of both Rousseau and Pestalozzi. He described the child's needs as being

- physical movement
- self or free activity and choice
- object work with real things (e.g. shells, cones, acorns)
- action and direct observation
- creativity through song, dance, drawing and three dimensional crafts
- nature study, gardening, cultivation and caring for living things.

And, most importantly, his aims were for the child to learn to live in society (of which the kindergarten provided a model) and to have teachers and parents as guides and helpers to learning

To support his methods, and to make the link between 'free' and 'natural' activities, Froebel created a series of specific, structured materials.

> In short sessions of directed play, the gifts were used to create pictures, or structures that fit loosely into three fundamental categories – forms of nature (or life), forms of knowledge (or science), and forms of beauty (or art).
>
> *Norman Brosterman, Inventing Kindergarten; Harry N Abrahams; 1997*

He called these 'Gifts and Occupations'. They are described in detail in *Inventing Kindergarten*. These 'gifts', in natural materials of wood, wool, clay and paper, were intended to work together through a series of free and adult-directed activities to expand and confirm children's sense of the pattern, order and beauty experienced in nature. The activities included building, weaving, sewing, cutting, folding, drawing

*Independent Learning in the Foundation Stage*

and modelling. All of these remain part of our early years curriculum today, both in child-initiated and adult-directed activities.

The influence of Froebel has been crucial to the emergence of the child-centred approach to early education. Froebel's ideas can be seen in action in, for example, the celebrated child-centred, play-based approaches of schools in Reggio Emilia in Italy, in the High/Scope movement in the USA and in quality nursery school practice in the UK. The best contemporary practitioners uphold the value of involvement, first hand experience, play and talk; and of the adult as co-worker with the child, supporting independence, curiosity and self motivation through sensitive and knowledgeable intervention.

> Play produces joy, freedom, satisfaction, repose both within and without, peace with the world. The springs of all good rest within it and go out from it. Exuberant curiosity is the most important learning asset.
>
> *Freidrich Froebel*

There are detailed descriptions of the Reggio and High/Scope approaches in Chapter 8.

## Into the 20th century

During the early part of the 20th century two important but conflicting influences on early education became apparent. On the one hand there was the emphasis on child development, the notion that children have clearly defined needs and interests which develop in a definable sequence; on the other, continuing support for an academic approach, emphasising curriculum content, standards of achievement and improvements in teaching. Readers will recognise that this tension still exists today, in some cases to the detriment of the experiences provided for children. We shall return to this in later chapters.

The emergence of psychology as a science in its own right, separate and distinct from its parent, philosophy, led to changes in focus. Psychologists recognised that the characteristics and behaviour of adults are rooted in their experiences as children. Child development, therefore, became a consuming interest of this new science. With this the emphasis changed from 'What is the right thing to do?', the question posed by philosophers, to 'What do people do?' And particularly, what do children do, why and at what stage?

## The developmental approach

Among the chief proponents of the developmental approach in the first part of the 20th Century were Freud and Piaget, and later Vygotsky and Bruner.

These thinkers and theorists were all interested in how children learn, how they build on early learning and at what stage they acquire the skills for independent learning. They based their work on extensive and painstaking observations of young children, at play and interacting with adults and each other. The outcome was a range of suggestions of structuring and referring to the processes of learning.

Sigmund Freud is best known as the founder of modern psychoanalysis. However, the more he explored the problems of adults, the greater became his interest in childhood and the formative influences on young children. He investigated links between gender, family relationships and the ability to learn. He was a pioneer in recognising stages of development, although he maintained that the influence of family is so strong that the progress through the stages of learning and the development of different parts of the personality are affected most of all by the quality of these early relationships. He held that the tension between the unconscious mind (which he termed the id), the conscious rational mind (the ego) and the moral mind (the superego) continues throughout life, and governs the development of conscious and unconscious thought, decision and action and, particularly relevant to our purposes, independence.

Jean Piaget constructed an account of the stages of development of children, which he proposed were common to everyone, universal and invariable. The child learns, he suggested, by continually constructing 'schemas'. A schema is a piece of knowledge about things themselves or, significantly, knowledge of how to do things. Schemas have been described by Cathy Nutbrown as 'repeatable patterns of behaviour, representation, speech and thought' with 'threads of thinking running through them'. Later stages revisit, re-work, test and extend the schemas developed in earlier ones. Piaget linked the developmental stages to broad age bands:

- the Sensory Motor Stage from birth to 18 months or so
- the Concrete Operations Stage from around two to about 11, divided into the Pre Operational Stage (from two to seven) and the Operational Period from seven to 11
- the Formal Operations Stage from about 12 onwards.

Piaget's observations led him to believe that children under seven, although learning fast about the social world, are unable to think or operate in a theoretical or independent way, or to work with abstract concepts such as space and time. However, more recent work in developmental psychology and investigation into brain function and development appear to challenge some of these assumptions.

*Independent Learning in the Foundation Stage*

'Schemas', first described by Piaget, are now accepted as a way of understanding and describing the way children make sense of their experiences and turn experience and action into thought. Thought is based on the internalisation and co-ordination of schemas, which have been explored through activity. Cathy Nutbrown, in her book *Threads of Thinking*, explains that schemas, or patterns of behaviour, speech, representation and thought can extend learning as they become established within a child's way of thinking.

> The newborn acts as if the world is centred about himself and must learn to behave in a more adaptive way. Similarly the young child thinks from a limited perspective and must widen it. Both infant and young child must de-centre (i.e. move away from a view of the world that is exclusively egocentric.
>
> *Jean Piaget*

We have all observed children becoming interested in and then often obsessed with particular conditions, objects or activities; for example, with enclosure, with circles, with verticals, with trajectory, as experienced in dropping something or throwing it. The unconscious thought is, 'Last time I did this, such and such happened. If I do it again, will it happen again?' Children are constantly hypothesising and testing in this way. Repetition reinforces the learning and creates paths for thinking (see *Again, Again!* A & C Black).

Lev Vygotsky, working in Russia at the turn of the last century (but not translated into English until the 1930's), and Jerome Bruner, working in the USA in the 1950s and 1960s, both explored the crucial relationship between language and learning, and the importance of sensitive intervention in the learning process by adults. They argued that it is through the acquisition of language that a child's understanding of his environment is transformed. The reports of their research emphasise the three aspects of interaction which are most important in the rapport between adult and child:

- sensitivity to the children
- stimulation of the children
- the ability to give children some degree of autonomy.

Readers will recognise these as principles adopted by the Effective Early Learning Project (1996).

Vygotsky describes the point of learning where the adult can be most effective as 'the zone of proximal or potential development' or ZPD. The ZPD is the gap that exists for an individual child between what she is capable of doing alone and what she can achieve with help from one more knowledgeable and skilled than herself. It is a point 'within the child's

> What a child can do with assistance today she will be able to do herself tomorrow.
>
> *Lev Vygotsky*

extended grasp', one that is almost beyond reach but not quite. The role of the adult (or a more competent peer) is to provide the support the child needs to reach out, stretch and seize this new element of knowledge or understanding. It is the stretching, the extending to the limits of one's capabilities, which for Vygotsky makes for the most effective learning.

Bruner added to this notion the view that any subject can be taught effectively in a sane, intellectual and honest form to any child at any stage of development. He conceived the curriculum as a spiral, containing points to be visited again and again at increasing levels of conceptual difficulty. This, he argued, enables a competent and informed practitioner to present any material in a context within the child's current level of understanding.

Bruner describes the role of the adult or peer in such learning as 'scaffolding', which he defines as making it possible 'for the child to internalise external knowledge and convert it into a tool for conscious control.' He warned against the assumption that the most effective scaffolding would be that provided by an adult; he was particularly impressed by the ability of children to co-teach each other through conversation and demonstration. It is in situations like this, he felt, when children are working alongside and with the help of their peers, that the most powerful learning takes place.

> Learning should not only take us somewhere; it should allow us later to go further more easily. The most sustained, productive conversations come from a pair of children working or playing together.
>
> *Jerome Bruner*

## Four more 20th century practitioners and their philosophies

An indication of the importance with which the education of young children is generally regarded is the fact that almost everyone has an opinion on how it should be done! Many early years practitioners, building on the work of Pestalozzi, Froebel and their contemporaries, developed views that reflected the continuing interest in how children learn and how best to help them. A range of differing approaches emerged, but when we look for references to independent learning some remarkable similarities can be seen. We have selected four of the most influential to discuss here.

Maria Montessori represents the point of view where children are seen as passive recipients of a rich, stimulating, formally organised setting. Margaret McMillan illustrates the Frobellian or 'nativist' view of the child in nature, exploring his environment, supported by a sensitive adult. Susan

Isaacs took from Freud, Froebel and Montessori and evolved a mixed culture, somewhere between freedom and structure. AS Neill, founder and leader of Summerhill School, epitomises the extreme in freedom. Building on Freud and Rousseau, he developed a purist view of the child as developing by taking responsibility for his or her own actions, learning and behaviour. Provided here is simply a taste of the style of each of these key figures, and a few words from each relating to independent learning. It cannot do more than cursory justice to the power of their own writing, to which the reader is referred.

Maria Montessori (1869-1952) trained as a doctor and specialised in working with socially and mentally handicapped children in Rome. She believed that the early stages of learning are the inevitable unfolding of a biological programme, and that within this programme there are special periods when the child is particularly receptive to the development of specific skills and activities. The nurseries that bear her name use a structured approach, employing a methodology where children learn from their own spontaneous actions but in a planned and structured environment, and often through a formal, pre-determined series of activities. Montessori placed an emphasis on real-life objects (furniture, crockery, tools) rather than toys and, unlike most practitioners, she saw no place for imaginative or free play, except within a planned and controlled environment as part of the child's progress towards autonomy.

> **Take certain objects and present them in a certain fashion, then leave the child alone with them and do not interfere.**
> *Maria Montessori*

Margaret McMillan (1860-1931) applied and built on the work of Frederick Froebel. Her approach was characterised by a continuing commitment to developing care and education side by side, with parents as partners and strong links between home and school. In her writings and practice she declared her view that play is a vehicle for education, emphasising free access to a setting which offered both indoor and outdoor environments.

> **Recognise the teachable moment and intervene at the appropriate time.**
> *Margaret McMillan*

She emphasised the value of imaginative play, and the importance of language, story and rhyme. Children should be free to choose their own activities and apparatus, learning to exercise responsible choice. The role of adults was to intervene in order to extend learning. She promoted and articulated the links between learning in the nursery garden and learning in the more formal subjects of the school curriculum (e.g. science, geography), and stressed the place of song, talk and story in developing literacy and music.

> Play with other children gives the child confidence in himself ...helping him discover the way in which he can carry out his own practical and imaginative pursuits with others, laying down the foundation for a co-operative social life in the later school years.
>
> *Susan Isaacs*

Susan Isaacs (1885-1948), who worked mainly in the independent sector, was influenced by Freud. She saw the promotion of the free expression of emotion as the way to support children's development. She combined the methodologies of Montessori and Froebel in an approach that balanced freedom with security, observing and recording what children did, and recognising the ability of young children to solve problems and think and reason in a logical way. Her methods and research directly challenged Piaget's view that very young children were egocentric and unable to reason. Making use of observations and examples from her own work and experience, she argued that even very young children are able to understand and to rationalise in ways that often surprise us.

AS Neill (1883-1973) was an ardent follower of Freud. A controversial figure throughout his life, he was seen by some as the high priest of freedom, which he promoted as the key to all educational growth. Many of his critics misunderstood the freedom enjoyed by children at Summerhill, his school, mistaking it for licence and seeing its practice as anarchy. In fact the approach at Summerhill emphasised control, but self control rather than control imposed from without. Neill believed that children develop if they are able to make decisions and choices, and that it was the job of educators to put them in situations which required this.

> By and large, parents should bestow as much responsibility as they can upon a child, with due regard for his physical safety. Only in this way will a parent develop the child's self-assurance.
>
> *AS Neill*

Their decisions and choices would inevitably sometimes be immature, and would be seen by some adults as 'wrong'. However, he had faith in the child as 'innately wise and realistic', and developed Summerhill as a place where a child was free to do 'anything which affects only him'. His opponents thought that he carried the notion of the child as a free agent too far, but Sir Herbert Read described AS Neill as 'bringing light and love into places where there was once tyranny and fear'.

These four thinkers and practitioners, so different in the detail of their approaches, nevertheless held significant principles in common, and these relate clearly to the child's developing independence. They can be summarised as:

– respect for the child

*Independent Learning in the Foundation Stage*

- the importance of observing children before intervening
- the development of independence through practical activities and play
- the centrality of choice
- the essential nature of hands-on experience
- the capacity of children to learn from each other and from sensitive adult interaction
- the requirement for practitioners to be knowledgeable and thoughtful about child development.

These principles offer a framework – an outline for creating a setting in which children can practice and learn independence. Later chapters will return to this framework and suggest ways in which it may be employed to create a rich and rewarding environment for learning. In concluding we invite readers to consider these questions.

- What are the pressures today that distract practitioners from the child-centred approach and principles promoted by the thinkers we have discussed in this chapter?
- How well are these principles upheld in your setting (or settings that you know)?
- Are they as obvious in the documents (e.g. aims, evaluation criteria) as they are in practice?
- What evidence would you look for in monitoring these aspects?

## Summary

The principles of independent learning have occupied the thoughts of early years educators and philosophers since the days of Rousseau in the early 18th century. Their aim has been 'developing the individual into a self-disciplined adult'.

Early years pioneers with different views and approaches agree on key principles. These are that:

- children learn best from hands-on experience and by using natural materials in a stimulating environment where work and play are all one
- learning should take place both indoors and out of doors
- the role of the adult is crucial
- we should always observe before intervening in children's learning
- children go through particular stages, and their learning will be affected by their current stage of development.

# Chapter 3:
# Recent knowledge and recent pressures

The context of education today is dominated by four important influences which hardly featured at all in earlier times. They are research, increased understanding, comparison and accountability.

When Rousseau devised an education for Emile the world was a very different place. Although the industrial revolution was under way, the pace of life and the expectations of the population were not very different from what they had been for centuries. By contrast, the 20th century was a time of great change, the pace of which accelerated in the years following the Second World War. Technological development, changes in patterns of employment and the working environment, increased mobility, the growth in the material wealth of many people living in the more affluent countries, the widespread instability of family and personal relationships were characteristics of the closing decades of the last century and have continued as features of the present one. These changes in our working and personal lives have had a profound effect.

> A revolution is changing your life – and your world. You are part of the first generation to live in a new age: an age that offers unlimited choice of futures in an era where virtually all things are possible. Your children's world will be like none other before. Their future, too, depends on their ability to grasp new conceptys, make new choices and go on learning and adapting throughout life.
>
> *Gordon Dryden and Jeannette Voss,*
> *The Learning Revolution; Network*
> *Education Press; 2005*

- **The increasing number of children whose parents go out to work**. Many children are now cared for in settings outside their own homes for part or all of the day. Universal pre-school provision is becoming common in many countries, and working parents are often too busy or too tired to play, cook or read with their children, leaving these crucial aspects of family life and child development to others.

- **The number of children living with only one of their parents**. Although in 2008, divorce was at its lowest for 28 years, this may be because fewer people are marrying in the first place! Whatever the reasons, this feature results in more children living in mixed, multiple or

single parent families, moving from parent to parent, group to group during the day and week, many spending less than two hours a week with a male relative (or male role model), and few encountering a male practitioner during their early years care and education.

- **The rise in the number of women living alone with their children.** The nuclear family is under threat. A society founded on married couples, with local grandparents and a network of family support on hand is part of history for many children. Not only does this often deprive them of contact with men, and their fathers in particular, it results in many inexperienced mothers who are thrust into the responsibilities of parenthood, sometimes before they have yet had time to reach maturity themselves.

- **A sedentary lifestyle is increasingly the norm** for adults and children alike. Children watch TV, use computers, play in their own rooms or in the rooms of other children, often with little supervision from or company with adults. Outdoor activity is often restricted, and there is a growing problem of child obesity.

  > We found every additional hour of TV exposure among toddlers corresponded to a future decrease in classroom engagement and success at math, increased victimization by classmates, have a more sedentary lifestyle, higher consumption of junk food and, ultimately, higher body mass index," says the study's lead author, *Dr. Linda S. Pagani; Quebec Longitudinal Study of Child Development; University of Montreal; 2010*

- **An increasingly protective environment**, where children are kept safe from all sorts of real or perceived dangers. Many young children never go out alone, even in their own gardens. Children are not encouraged to play in the street or the local parks and fields. Many children are now frightened to be alone, they spend less time out of doors in natural light, and for many children, night-time darkness is unfamiliar. Fear in adults has reduced opportunities for outdoor play, shopping is a more popular weekend activity than walking in the park or visiting the country. If children are involved in activities or friendships outside their own home they are taken and fetched by adults, even over a very short distance.

  > For children, nature comes in many forms. A newborn calf; a pet that lives and dies; a worn path through the woods; a fort nested in stinging nettles; a damp, mysterious edge of a vacant lot – whatever shape nature takes, it offers each child an older, larger world separate from parents.
  >
  > *Richard Louv, Last Child in the Woods; Atlantic Books; 2010*

  - The increasingly protective environment is often a response to living in **a more overtly violent society**. Even in homes

where violent behaviour rarely occurs, children from an early age see adults being angry and violent towards each other on TV; outbursts described by Daniel Goleman as resulting from 'increased emotional ineptitude, desperation and recklessness in our families, our communities and our collective lives.'

- **Children's health is increasingly affected by our environment**. More children have allergies. Asthma and eczema have increased significantly over the past decade and continue to do so. Reactions to foods, drugs and the environment have been shown to have a striking affect on behaviour. We also live in a society where processed and ready-prepared food is easily available and cheap; where eating is more a fuelling operation and less of a social occasion; and where many of the 'junk foods' that children so love contain artificial colourings and additives, some of which can have dramatic and alarming effects on behaviour and health.

- **We have lively media which apparently revel in bad news**. We have also developed a culture where the consumer is king – or queen – and complaint is encouraged. Out of this has grown a public delight in seeing professionals get it wrong. We live in an era of public service accountability, and the education services have not escaped. On the whole this is an excellent thing; those who work with other people's children and who provide an essential service for which those people are paying, whether in the public or the private sector, should rightly be accountable. However, there is a down side of accountability as the curriculum for the early years has become more clearly described and outcomes and targets identified. The features of effective teaching are examined and reported in public documents, practitioners are scrutinised, observed and inspected in a way that has never happened before. All this can inhibit spontaneous responses to children's interests, as practitioners and teachers doggedly stick to what they have planned, thus reducing opportunities for independent learning.

> The ability to control impulse is the base of will and character. The root of altruism lies in empathy, the ability to read emotions in others. And if there are any two moral stances that our times call for, they are precisely these: self-restraint and compassion.
>
> *Goleman, Emotional Intelligence; Bloomsbury; 1996*

While we all recognise the reasons for such changes, and let us not forget that many of them have also a beneficial side, the effect on children's independence and autonomy is profound. Often the only place where children are safe and free to experiment and plan their own activities is in their early years setting. The responsibility for practitioners is to provide opportunities for this; the

responsibility for parents is to recognise and support the practitioners' commitment to active and autonomous learning.

In the 2001 RSA Jigsaw Lecture, Professor Colin Blakemore of Oxford University said: *'Whatever is the cause, there is an escalating, self-reinforcing problem of a breakdown of society, a lack of understanding of the needs of others, of the benefits of collaboration, of responsibility, of social conscience, and I think that those are things that children are normally programmed to learn between the ages of two, three, four and five. If it's not happening in the home – and I'm afraid we have to admit that increasingly it is not – then we have to see, and I think formally acknowledge that it is the responsibility of our school system to substitute for what homes are no longer giving adequately to a large fraction of our kids, and to seize the opportunity of these extra years (the Early Years Foundation Stage) to design a curriculum which will build kids who have a better sense of self in relation to others and who know the value of altruism, co-operation, collaboration and social duty.'*

The implication for educators is clear – we must rethink most of our existing educational paradigms, for they are based on views of society that are no longer valid. Students must be prepared to accept, adapt to, and thrive upon change. The process of education must deal with the needs of students to develop both macro and micro strategies for dealing with their world.

L Tsantis, Creating the Future, Technology as the Catalyst; www.newhorizons.org

However, we are all under pressure to work faster, do better, meet targets for improvement and test our effectiveness. The result can be a restricted curriculum, narrowed opportunities, and children who, like George, our second example in Chapter 1, learn helplessness at an early stage.

A way of coping with this maze of demands and expectations is to stand back from the day-to-day pressures of our jobs and try to do two things:

1.  Find out what we now know about how children learn, the way their brains develop and the best ways to help them, and
2.  Use this information to strengthen our resolve to do what we know is right for the children in our care.

In the remainder of this chapter we explore some of the most recent findings on the working of the human brain and how it develops, and suggest how best to use this knowledge to help children's learning. We also look at the implications of the age of accountability; the effect of a National Curriculum, with measurable indicators, where settings, schools, regions and nations can be compared. And we look at how the discussion of methodologies, practices and principles has re-kindled interest in the way young children learn, and the best way to support them.

# What we now know about how the brain works

Nearly everything we know about the brain we've learned in the last 25 years.

*Dryden & Voss, The New Learning Revolution; Network Education Press; 2005*

We learn 10% of what we read, 15% of what we hear, but 80% of what we experience. Neural connections that don't develop in the first five years of life may never develop at all.

*Dryden & Voss, Ibid.*

During the second half of the 20th century there was an unprecedented increase in research and the resulting information about brain development – how the brain physically develops and, as importantly, how thinking develops. Most of what we know about the brain has been discovered in the last 25 years, and the outcomes of this research are staggering in their implications. Let us offer you some of them, taken from books identified in our bibliography. They are generalisations, but are no less arresting for that.

We now know that:

- children who have experienced a rich range of sensory experiences in their first year will have laid down more complex neural networks than children who have not been so stimulated.
- children who watch TV for more than six hours a day are more likely to do less well at school than those who watch for less than two hours per day. However, we also know that children who watch for up to two hours a day are better informed, have livelier imaginations and are likely to be more literate. (*Quebec Longitudinal Study of Child Development; University of Montreal; 2010*)
- there is a measurable connection between active learning (physical play, make believe, word play) and brain growth.
- within the first four years children: learn two thousand words, double their brain size from birth, develop 50% of their eventual ability to think (sometimes called their intelligence) and develop preferences for activity and learning which are physically based and gender related.
- young boys are more likely to be competitive, physical, active and independent, to like numbers, constructions and objects, and tend to move frequently from activity to activity, because throughout early childhood they are dominated by the active, right half of their brains. Young girls are more likely to be verbal and co-operative, to have a preference for books, drawing, paint, and to be able to concentrate, because, at a young age, they are able to access both sides of their brains. We were aware of these behaviours before. Now we are beginning to understand the reasons for them.

*Independent Learning in the Foundation Stage*

- the complex skills of reading and writing (concentration, hand/eye co-ordination, an interest in language, etc.) rely on the development of links between the left and the right sides of the brain. These links develop in girls at around the age of four, and in boys rather later, often as late as six or even seven. We also know that five times as many boys as girls have significant reading problems at eight. The question we must ask is – are we pushing boys into failure situations by trying to teach them to read and write when the physical development of their brains and bodies is not yet mature enough to cope with such complex tasks?

> Children are not blank tablets or unbridled appetites or even intuitive seers. Babies and young children think, observe and reason. They consider evidence, draw conclusions, do experiments, solve problems and search for the truth.
>
> *Alison Gopnik, Andrew Meltzoff and Patricia Kuhl; How Babies Think; Phoenix; 2001*

During the recent period of extensive research into the way the brain works, there have been some significant landmarks, which can help us in our thinking and our practice. One of these was a discovery that, far from being 'empty vessels waiting to be filled', babies and young children are confident, capable thinkers, with complex brain patterns already present in their brains, created before birth and from their earliest days.

Margaret Donaldson's influential work *Children's Minds* was published in Britain in 1978, and her radical propositions concerning the way children think challenged the findings of Piaget. Donaldson asserted that children are already skilled thinkers and users of language by the time they go to school. Far from being those egocentric thinkers in Piaget's observations, children as young as three can appreciate other points of view if problems are carefully explained to them and placed in a familiar context. She also explored children's ability to reason, and the crucial relationship between language development and all the other features of the child's mental growth.

> There is a fundamental human urge to be effective, competent and independent, to understand the world and act with skill.
>
> *Margaret Donaldson, Children's Minds; HarperCollins; 1986*

In an echo of Vygotsky's ZPD, explained in the last chapter, the research studied and interpreted by Donaldson indicated that a crucial task for the practitioner in the early years is to guide the child towards things he can do well, but not too easily, assessing his skills, understanding his confidence and responding to his errors in helpful ways. In *Children's Minds*, she includes a quotation from the poet Gerard Manley Hopkins: 'There is a point within me in matters of any size, when I must absolutely have encouragement as much as crops rain ... Afterwards I

*Recent knowledge and recent pressures*

> If a child is going to control and direct his own thinking ... he must become conscious of it.
> *Margaret Donaldson, Children's Minds; HarperCollins; 1986*

am independent.' She also discusses the tension for teachers between freedom and control. Schools and settings are social organisations which require rules and order to function properly. However, one of the ways children develop independence of mind is by experimenting with rules and order. They need a structured environment for learning, where they are respected, where they are not afraid of failure, are 'offered opportunities to learn, to ask their own questions, to express themselves spontaneously and be unconstrained.'

At about the same time as Donaldson was developing her ideas, Howard Gardner was working in America to identify a range of forms of intelligence and to challenge traditional approaches to schooling. Many teachers and parents have observed the ways in which children might achieve highly in one area but less well in others. Gardner postulated that there are different types of learners and thinkers, and that these are linked to different types of intelligence, and the seven key intelligences he names are mathematical/ logical, linguistic, visual/spatial, musical, interpersonal, intrapersonal and kinaesthetic, each present in us all, but with peaks and troughs in each individual. In doing so he fuelled a worldwide debate about the nature of learning. This debate contrasts features of early years education accepted by practitioners since the days of Froebel and Pestalozzi what we have discovered about the brain in the last 25 years with.

> Education should try to preserve the most remarkable features of the young mind – its adventurousness, its generativity, its resourcefulness, and its flashes of flexibility and creativity.
> *Howard Gardner, The Unschooled Mind; Basic Books; 1993*

Accelerated Learning methods linked the new knowledge and understanding of the brain and how it develops with techniques for successful learning. Some of the methods suggested may be seen as common sense and have been known and used by good teachers for many years.

They have been promoted by Tony Buzan, and embedded in practice in some schools by Alistair Smith. The proponents of Accelerated Learning offer a curriculum that, as well as building specific basic academic, physical and artistic abilities, stresses:

- enjoyment in learning
- high self esteem
- the importance of training in life skills
- the importance of children 'learning how to learn'.

The Accelerated Learning approach supports the view that 'our homes, beaches, forests, playgrounds, zoos, museums and adventure areas are the world's best schools' (Dryden & Voss).

The echoes of Rousseau and all those who followed him still resound as practitioners discuss methodology in the early years, and the schools where informed principles survive against the odds of current pressures are those which we now hold up as examples of quality practice.

In 1996 Daniel Goleman published a now best-selling work on the links between emotional engagement and learning. He called it *Emotional Intelligence*, making the point that learning how to manage and direct the emotions is as important as learning how to use the intellect or motor skills. This thinking advanced Howard Gardner's work by presenting a new view of the intelligences he had identified in *Frames of Mind*.

Goleman argued that the growth of all the intelligences is rooted in the emotions, and he suggested that the 'eighth intelligence', emotional intelligence is the most important key to adult success and happiness, the factor which has been most neglected in recent years. Its lack, he says, results in 'surging rage and despair, whether in the quiet loneliness of latchkey kids left with the TV for a babysitter, or in the pain of children abandoned, neglected or abused, or in the ugly intimacy of marital violence.'

> The importance of the research is that the brain is plastic. What we have here is an opportunity with children to make a huge difference by being systematic in the way that we provide stimulation. The brain is growing faster at that point than it ever will again in the child's lifetime. We can boost that growth curve by increasing the amount of stimulation by light, sound, touch, movement and the contents.
>
> *Daniel Goleman, Emotional Intelligence; Bloomsbury; 1996*

As well as exploring brain structure and development, Goleman addresses what it means to be emotionally intelligent. He discusses the way a child deficient in emotional intelligence is at risk as he or she grows up. He points out how many of the dysfunctions of contemporary society can be linked to immature and undernourished emotions. He also suggests what schools can do to 'educate the whole student, bringing together mind and heart in the classroom.' He includes examples of school programmes for encouraging emotional intelligence, and the results of research into their effectiveness.

Goleman concludes that effective programmes for developing emotional intelligence in children aged five to 11 need to include key elements grouped into emotional, cognitive and behavioural skills. Further research showed that in comparison with control schools, children who have experienced systematic teaching of these skills demonstrate impressive improvements.

These children prove to:

- be more responsible
- be more assertive
- be more popular and outgoing
- be more pro-social and helpful
- have better understanding of others
- be more considerate and concerned
- have more pro-social strategies for interpersonal problem solving
- be more harmonious
- be more democratic
- be better able to resolve conflict.

What are the implications of this research for the way practitioners teach and support the children they work with? How should they recognise and provide for the different ways of learning and differences in intelligences in their groups? How do they counteract the less desirable influences of modern life on the children they work with?

*A massive survey of parents and teachers shows a worldwide trend for the present generation of children to be more troubled emotionally than the last; more lonely and depressed, more angry and unruly, more nervous and prone to worry, more impulsive and aggressive.*

*Daniel Goleman, Emotional Intelligence; Bloomsbury; 1996*

Each of the educational innovators whose contributions we have discussed has worked with principles developed from a passionate interest in children and the way they learn, and with a conviction that early childhood is a special period with its own needs and rights, and not just a preparation for the next stage of the person's development. Their conviction is now supported by the research into the human brain, where all the evidence confirms that first hand experience in a context of play, talk and the presence of high quality adult support are still the keys to successful learning, and that what is experienced in the first few years of life will determine not only what we learn, but how we learn, how much we learn and how we can use what we learn.

So why are we all still debating the methodology for nurturing the emerging skills of independent thinking and learning, which are at the heart of educational history? Why are we not doing what has been shown to be correct and what we know is right?

## The pressures of innovation

During the last quarter of the 20th century, education, and early years education in particular, has experienced unprecedented upheaval and

turmoil. We have been subjected to initiatives from successive governments, the introduction of national systems for accountability and a high level of public interest. National programmes often produced mixed messages, creating stress and confusion. Practitioners in the United Kingdom, as elsewhere, were bombarded with a plethora of guidance on the nature and purposes of the early years curriculum:

> Of the 19 countries (included on the INCA database) for which evidence was available, 13 had national early years curriculum guidelines, while six countries did not. Those countries which did not have these guidelines were generally those with a state, regional or federal system where responsibility for early years education and care was devolved to this second tier of government. In these countries, there were state-level curriculum guidelines available, which early years settings across the public, private and voluntary sectors were expected to use in the development of their individualised programmes.
>
> *Tony Bertram, Chris Pascal; Early Years Education: An International Perspective; Centre for Research in Early Childhood, Birmingham; QCDA/NFER; 2002*
> *www.inca.org.uk*

In England these initiatives and reports have included The Rumbold Report, Starting with Quality (1990), First Class (1993), The Dearing Report (1993), Quality in Diversity (1998), Desirable Outcomes for Children's Learning (1998) the QCA Guidance on the Foundation Curriculum (2000), Birth to Three Matters (2002), and most recently, The Early Years Foundation Stage for children from birth to five (2008). Each of these documents, while containing many valuable ideas and upholding the accepted principles of early years education, proposed different ways of structuring experiences and different ways of characterising excellence.

During this time, practitioners, writers and researchers have added their voices to the debate about approaches. Tina Bruce, Audrey Curtis, Janet Moyles, Chris Pascall, Kathy Sylva and many others have observed and interpreted learning in the early years, identifying and recording the curriculum in action, promoting the view that play is the best way to 'learn how to learn'. They also present a unified voice in talking about independent learning as 'the source of technological innovation so necessary for our economic survival', while emphasising

**Children are competent learners from birth and develop and learn in a wide variety of ways. All practitioners should, therefore, look carefully at the children in their care, consider their needs, their interests, and their stages of development and use all of this information to help plan a challenging and enjoyable experience across all the areas of Learning and Development.**

*EYFS Statutory Framework; DCSF; May 2008*

the need to protect early childhood as 'a stage in its own right, not just as a preparation for adulthood'. Both the National Curriculum and the QCA Guidance for the Foundation Stage have contained explicit recommendations on the promotion of independent learning as an essential element of personal and social education.

The guidance on the Foundation Stage Curriculum (EYFS) has stimulated a debate about planning. Conscientious practitioners in all sectors of early years provision have always planned the environment and the experiences offered, and some have involved the children in this planning. However, the message practitioners have received (from their own observation of teachers in schools, as well as from some inspectors and advisers) is this: planning means writing, and writing means deciding well before the event what children will do. The danger then is that the needs and preferences of children become overridden by the plan. The plan becomes the focus, rather than the learning. Practitioners may well feel, 'If I have written this plan in my own spare time, the children will have those experiences, whatever emerges as their real preference or need!' We are not against planning. Planning is essential to ensure that children experience range and balance. But over-rigid planning leads to too much emphasis on adult-directed and adult-led tasks, and too little emphasis on independent, child-initiated learning. This is despite the fact that the QCA/DfES guidance explicitly advocates a good balance between adult-directed and child-initiated activities.

Each of the new reforms brought its own structures, regulatory bodies and systems for quality assurance and accountability. Practitioners are encouraged to review, monitor and account for the quality of their settings, using a range of instruments. Performance Management and Effective Early Learning (EEL), and new guidance from inspection offer valuable and first hand opportunities for practitioners to carry out extensive evaluation of their own practice in order to recognise success and identify targets for improvement. They do, however, add to the paperwork and the growing discussion about workload.

From the perspective of the setting or its play area it has often seemed that the turmoil of innovation has inhibited rather than enhanced the maintenance of an appropriately independent environment for young learners. Practitioners are caught at the heart of this tension – on one hand they welcome the focus on education, on early learning in particular, and on

> **The EYFS requires providers to ensure a balance of child-initiated and adult-led play-based activities. Providers should use their judgement and their knowledge of the children in their care in deciding what the balance should be.**
>
> *EYFS Statutory Framework; DCSF; May 2008*

*Independent Learning in the Foundation Stage*

providing clear guidance on common features of good practice. On the other hand they feel under enormous pressure to perform according to some national blueprint for excellence, on which they will be tested and held accountable. They feel that the demands of accountability and paperwork inevitably take them away from the core purposes of their work – observing and interacting with children. One young teacher summed up anxieties felt by many: 'Yes, but suppose the children don't initiate what I need them to in order to learn what they have to?' Is it any wonder that even experienced early years practitioners are confused and lacking confidence? Practitioners who know what children need feel cautious and anxious about providing it. Why should it be so difficult to do what we know is right?

> Play underpins all development and learning for young children. Most children play spontaneously, although some may need adult support, and it is through play that they develop intellectually, creatively, physically, socially and emotionally.
>
> *EYFS Statutory Framework; DCSF; May 2008*

In 1997, the feelings of two experienced Reception teachers in a primary school involved in the EEL Project were described like this: 'Recent changes, mostly emanating from outside the school, had left them less sure about their abilities and they worried that they often were being asked to do things which they felt were not suited to the needs of their children. They were losing confidence, and their commitment to the system – although not to the children – had become increasingly doubtful ... The management of the school perceived the 'real business' of the reception class to be predominantly cognitive development, and this should be narrowed down more prescriptively to focus on objectives – a reality which was very different from the rhetoric of the school's public statements.'

Following the introduction of the early years Foundation Stage in 2008, the government produced a huge range of resources and initiatives to support the principles it enshrined. The questions asked by practitioners were answered in printed documents, DVD, website chat-rooms and national and regional conferences. A consistent message about child-initiated learning, and the way practitioners could support this in 'playful adult-led activities' was promoted, and used by many practitioners to overhaul their adult dominated practice in favour of child-initiated learning and the following of children's interests.

However, tension still remained! Some practitioners (and their managers) were still open to pressure to raise standards, and an assumption that formality was the way to do this.

# Seven areas of pressure

Of course, one way of dealing with pressure is to face up to it and organise it. These are the areas of pressure identified by practitioners, and some ways of coping with them.

### 1. We are all so different
The range of settings within the early years is enormous – from the childminder in a network to the Reception class in a large primary school; from the pre-school in multi-use accommodation, where every piece of equipment must be put out at the beginning of each session and put away again at the end, to the purpose-built nursery. The range of qualifications in these settings is also huge. For example, the management of the education workforce is resulting in some cases in the drafting into the Foundation Stage of teachers whose entire training and careers have been with a different age group. Working towards a consistent model of good practice will take time, effort and training. Meanwhile, there is still a danger that the practical nature of the curriculum will be lost and the experiences of the children impoverished.

### 2. Children spend different lengths of time with us
The age at which children start the Foundation Stage and the length of time they spend in it depends on when they were born and where they live. There is still little recognition of the implications of this for the mental and emotional growth of children and their subsequent progress through the education system.. The balance of time spent in statutory provision (e.g. in nursery or reception classes) and in voluntary, private or independent settings (e.g. in pre-schools, playgroups, private nurseries, with childminders) also varies greatly from area to area and child to child. This makes matching opportunities to abilities even more complex, especially when national indicators are usually age related.

### 3. What is happening to the statutory school age?
In many countries, the curriculum for three to six year olds now straddles compulsory and non-compulsory phases of education. In England, children reach their entitlement to statutory schooling the term after their fifth birthday. The last year of the Foundation Stage is often described as the reception year, since most children are admitted to the reception class of an infant or primary school at some point during that year. However, there is a continuing debate about the appropriate age for children to start formal school, and a general feeling that a more appropriate age for this might be

*Independent Learning in the Foundation Stage*

the end of the reception year, thus bringing the UK into line with most European countries.

Practitioners working with children in the year before statutory school age are still under pressure from a range of quarters to meet inappropriate targets for the National Curriculum, rather than meeting the needs of individual children by recognising their stage of development, not merely their chronological age. The emphasis when requesting pre-school information, and the subsequent setting of targets for learning, is often on literacy and numeracy, with personal and social education, play and independence given much less weight.

## 4. What about mixed-age classes?
Across the UK many classes in maintained schools cater for children in the early years alongside those in Key Stage 1. There has been research and training on the issues of continuity and progression between non-statutory and statutory stages of education, whether it is across settings, across classes or even in the same class.

> A high quality early years experience provides a firm foundation on which to build future academic, social and emotional success. Key to this is ensuring continuity between all settings and that children's social, emotional and educational needs are addressed appropriately.
> *EYFS Practitioner Guidance; DCSF; May 2008*

## 5. What about the effects of the recent initiatives to raise standards?
In many countries the early years curriculum has been seen as a way to improve standards, particularly for those children in less affluent circumstances. An additional impetus has been the need and desire for women to go out to work, which has resulted in a substantial increase in funding for early years provision.

> Perceptions of quality vary between national contexts, but evidence of the social and economic benefits has been a major factor in the recent introduction of regulatory frameworks including pre-school education, which vary according to these perceptions. *Tony Bertram, Chris Pascal; Early Years Education: An International Perspective; Centre for Research in Early Childhood, Birmingham; QCDA/NFER; 2002 www.inca.org.uk*

In England, the acknowledgement of the importance of high quality early years provision in raising standards later in life, has resulted in many initiatives, some of which have threatened the place of independent learning at the heart of the early years curriculum. The structure of some of these programmes is based on age related indicators and takes little account of

*Recent knowledge and recent pressures*

> Throughout the Foundation Phase, children should be given opportunities to develop their skills, knowledge and understanding through being involved in a range of experiences including different types of play and a range of planned activities that allow them to become independent learners.
>
> *Framework for Children's Learning for 3 to 7-year-olds in Wales; Department for Children, Education, Lifelong Learning and Skills; 2008*

children's stages of development, or the latest research on the development of the brain. Practitioners have been strongly encouraged to pursue methods for the teaching of literacy and numeracy which conflict with what we know about early development. This 'top-down' pressure is evident in many countries where the standards agenda has overtaken the research evidence about early learning.

In Wales, the devolved government have taken a different approach. The Foundation Phase here extends beyond statutory school age and includes the first two years of the primary curriculum, emphasising the importance of continuity in practice for young learners.

### 6. How do we convince parents that an emphasis on a more practical approach is right for their children?

Parents' expectations are more clear since the introduction of national guidance for the early years, and this sometimes makes them more focused on the *standards* achieved by their children, rather than the *quality* of their experience. Parents also feel that early years experience in a pre-school, playgroup or nursery is somehow different from the experience in a school, and as children move into school, parents expect 'play' to stop and 'work' to start; this perception has only been reinforced by the pressure on the school curriculum of an emphasis on outcome indicators.

Most parents want their children to be happy in school, but their expectations are now often linked with an academic target reached or a National Curriculum level gained. Differing expectations of different types of setting still remain, and there is a perception that 'school is best', despite the evidence from research that children gain the greatest long term benefit from time spent in nursery settings and in designated nursery classes in infant or primary schools.

### 7. How are we going to manage the new environment, in a time of international economic turmoil, while ensuring high standards in all?

The expansion of funded places available for under-fives and the encouragement of diversity in provision have resulted in a wide variation in standards, approaches, methodology and staff training. We are now in a

*Independent Learning in the Foundation Stage*

time of stress. High unemployment, financial difficulties for parents, cuts in public services and, in the UK, a growing school population resulting from economic migration will all contribute to pressure on early years provision. Even within the same setting the quality of the provision caries from room to room and even from one part of the day to another. Take this range and apply it across a nation, or the western world as a whole, and you have a volatile mixture of pressures for flexible provision and a focus on value for money.

While applauding the principle of equal access to early education, we must continue to hope that the current unevenness in quality across and within nations is a short-term problem. The provision of common frameworks for the curriculum and the increase of joint training has gone only part of the way in addressing this issue.

Charles Handy, writer and thinker, said of managing change:

> 'If anything is to happen ... it has to start with us, individually, in our own place and time. To wait for a leader to guide us into the future is to be forever disillusioned.' *Charles Handy; The Empty Raincoat; Random House; 1995*

We would only add that looking at the children you work with, finding out what they already know and can do, and planning to meet their needs will help you to find that place to start.

## Summary

Brain research has shown us the importance of the early years in establishing what sort of person we grow up to be, both intellectually and emotionally.

Children learn more in the first five years of life than they will ever learn again.

Pressures of accountability have resulted in a narrowing of the curriculum for some under-fives. They have become more dependent on adults, more passive in their learning, and many are experiencing more direct teaching and less of the explorative learning necessary at this stage. The introduction of guidance for education in the early years can and should be used to defend the rights of young children to develop all aspects of learning in a way that is appropriate to their age and stage of development.

# Section 2

Developing
Independent
Learners

# Chapter 4:
# What helps a child to become an independent learner?

What are the essential skills and attributes which support independent learning?

How does independence develop? What are the key events and what can adults do to help?

This chapter explores the nature and development of independence in young children. It includes descriptions of the aptitudes and skills associated with the child's developing independence from a range of perspectives, and the key stages in the emergence of independence from birth to five/six years old.

## What is an independent learner?

A good place to start exploring a 'What is...?' question is a dictionary. A dictionary definition of independent is: 'autonomous; not depending on authority or control; self-governing; not depending on another person for one's opinion.' A dictionary definition of autonomous is: 'acting independently or having the freedom to do so.'

Quality in Diversity (1998) described the process of becoming independent through play like this: 'By their play, children are learning about themselves, about who they are and what they might become. They experiment with what they can do without fear of failure. They develop confidence, a sense of self worth and identity. They make and break their own rules. They try out different roles, explore and challenge stereotypes. They learn to communicate with increasing skill and confidence.'

One of the four key themes of the early years Foundation Stage (2008) in England is 'Positive Relationships – children learn to be strong and independent from a base of loving and secure relationships with parents and/or a key person.'

Practitioners should regularly confirm their commitment to independent learning and children's autonomy, both as a monitoring activity and in re-establishing the aims for their setting in meeting the needs of every child.

Identifying the key skills and attributes of independence can be a useful starting point in a review of your current practice.

We asked a number of practitioners and others with experience of young people to list the qualities and describe the behaviours which were characteristic of young independent learners. The collection is not an exhaustive one, it is an attempt to define some of the qualities, skills and attitudes which many parents and most practitioners seek to encourage in children, and value when they see them. The list which follows could provide a framework for review or a checklist for improvement which can be used by an individual or applied across a setting or school. Making regular reference to such descriptions may help you in evaluating your work.

An independent learner...

### ... asks questions
S/he is a child who is interested in everything and wants to know more, asking relevant questions and taking real notice of the answers.

### ... is a problem solver
S/he is a child who shows initiative, thinks things out and tries new solutions, learning from mistakes and errors.

### ... is a creative thinker
S/he is a child who uses equipment, resources, language and people in a creative way, combining materials and methods or using language in unusual ways, constructing things and developing ideas.

### ... is confident
S/he is a child who relates easily to adults and other children, is not afraid to try new things, speak to a group of known companions, choose a new activity.

### ... can make choices
S/he is a child who can consider options, take time to choose, articulate needs and sustain interest in a chosen activity.

### ... has a positive, 'can do' attitude
S/he is a child who will 'have a go', will take reasonable risks, copes well with initial failure on the way to success.

### ... makes learning links
S/he is a child who makes connections, sees relationships and links personal experiences into real learning.

### ... is self motivated
S/he is an intrinsically motivated 'self starter', a child who does not need encouragement to get involved in learning.

### ... has high self esteem and a good self image
S/he is a child with a good opinion of his or her own worth, who values family, community and culture and who confidently expects to do well.

### ... helps others
S/he is a child who readily helps others in the setting, offering assistance and support to younger or less confident children, and is willing to share responsibility with them.

### ... sets their own goals
S/he is a child with clear intentions and a good idea of how they can be achieved; s/he works hard at each stage to carry them out, while being open to adjustments and rethinking.

### ... wants to understand
S/he is a child who is evidently engaging with the world, who is working hard at learning.

### ... wants to achieve
S/he is a child who enjoys learning for its own sake, not just to please an adult, who sustains attention and concentration, who adapts and adjusts when things go wrong and who uses people, materials, books, ICT, to help in learning and to pursue interests.

### ... uses teachers and other adults
S/he is a child who readily and easily turns to the adults in the setting and at home to help with and join in learning.

### ... can find and select their own materials
S/he is a child who shows initiative; who does not wait to be given materials and equipment but selects and organises space and apparatus with clear purposes in mind.

### ... has interested parents who give encouragement at and from home
S/he is a child who receives a single message from the adults in his or her life – a message of support, encouragement and value for what they have tried to do and what they have achieved.

Most early years practitioners and many parents would probably come up with similar lists. The attributes, qualities and skills identified here are familiar to us all and are surely what we all want to see for all children. They would be as recognisable and supported by the educationalists celebrated in Chapter 2 as they are by you today.

Independent learners get deeply involved in learning, often entering the 'flow' experience described by Mihalyi Csikszentmihalyi, professor of

Human Development and Education at Chicago University as the state where time seems to stand still and self-consciousness disappears as the child becomes totally absorbed in the activity:

> The flow experience acts as a magnet for learning. *Mihalyi Csikszentmihalyi; Flow: The Psychology of Happiness; Rider; 2002*

However, these personal characteristics, and the climate where 'flow' can flourish do not emerge in every setting or in every child unless we first identify them, accept their value, and put in place a framework that will help them to grow. We must then trust the children to manage their own activities and any risks these might involve, and identify and concentrate on the things that are important to them. Doing this will affect the whole context of your work - the style of teaching and learning in your setting, the organisation of the resources, the pattern of the day, the grouping of the children, the role of the adults and your relationships with parents.

## How does independence develop?

Before moving on to how we encourage and support the independent learner, it is helpful to spend some time reviewing how independence develops in the early years.

Evidence from research confirms what we have all experienced and observed; children need and rely on parents, or parent substitutes, particularly when they are very young. Without them they may fail to play, to sleep well or to make good relationships with others later in life. During the first three months of life, a baby is more likely to cry if alone than when near her mother. She is least likely to cry when actually being held by her mother. Mothers have a biological need to be near their babies, and babies need to be near their mothers. Each one is anxious when the other is out of sight.

John Bowlby warned that children are in danger of failing to develop healthy relationships in later years if they lack warm and continuing attachment when they are young. More recent research indicates that in order to flourish children do not need to be with their own parent for every moment of every day, and that children can relate to several parent figures or carers equally. However, the

> **Knowing that adults, space, time and materials will be constant, the same today as yesterday, helps young children to assume more responsibility for what they do and to follow their own threads of thinking and doing without unnecessary hindrance or over-dependence on adults.**
>
> *Cathy Nutbrown, Threads of Thinking; Sage; 2011*

relationship between babies and their parents (or parent figures) is the single most important influence on their growth and development, for at least the first year of their lives.

From his research, including interviews with children, Jean Piaget developed theories of learning and a developmental progression which had a major influence on thinking during the 20th Century. Chapter 2 introduced two major threads which are particularly relevant to the subject of this book. The first of these is the principle of schemas or mental structures, which help children to adapt to and learn from their environment. The second is that children progress through a sequence of stages of development. These stages are loosely associated with age bands, but Piaget stressed that different children may move from stage to stage at different ages.

The main developmental stages Piaget identified in children under seven are:

## Stage 1 - the sensory motor period (before the age of two)

Piaget proposed that babies are born with schemas or instinctive patterns of behaviour for sucking, grasping, etc., and that these are at the centre of their development during the first two years. During this time they depend on adult carers for all their needs, and the simple schemas are triggered and reinforced through feeding, cuddling and becoming familiar with objects and events. As young babies explore, experiment, practise and begin to make sense of the detail of objects and events, they gain more knowledge and understanding of the world around them. In

doing so they adapt and develop their simple schemas to accommodate their new experiences.

A first independent activity for babies is often a treasure basket which enables them to select objects for themselves as they focus on these repetitive behaviours, such as filling and emptying containers, patting, banging and manipulating the objects.

## Stage 2 - the pre-operational period (between the ages of about two and seven)

By the age of two children have had a wide experience of objects and activities. However, Piaget suggested that children in the pre-operational

*Independent Learning in the Foundation Stage*

stage have not yet established the differences between animate and inanimate objects. Animism – attributing life to inanimate objects – is a predominant feature of this stage. A young child who could not remove her shoe exclaimed in exasperation, 'Let go, shoe!' The child who falls will blame the table for bumping his head. These behaviours are typical of the animism characteristic of this stage.

Piaget believed that pre-operational children, although more aware of themselves as individuals, are generally unable to take into account the point of view of others around them. In the early part of this stage a child will play alone or in parallel with other children, even when in a group. Later on she will join in with others as they play, but her egocentricity will encourage her to dominate the situation and this will often result in friction as individuals jockey for position in the group. Piaget always maintained that children under seven are physiologically and psychologically unable to take another's point of view into account.

In early years settings the adults are encouraged to take on the role of the parent during these two stages of a child's development.

> **A key person will help the baby or child to become familiar with the setting and to feel confident and safe within it.**
>
> *Practitioner Guidance for the EYFS;*
> *DCSF; 2008*

In Chapter 3 we noted that more recent experts in child development, such as Margaret Donaldson and Daniel Goleman, have questioned some of Piaget's conclusions about the behaviour of children at the pre-operational stage. There is now evidence that children's ability to empathise and see other people's points of view emerges much earlier than Piaget thought.

Recent research has helped us to construct a more precise sequence of emotional and behavioural development, bearing in mind that relating these to ages will always be fraught with difficulty and danger! In an attempt to head off controversy and dissent we want to establish two key points.

1. **Children differ.** The elements of independence appear at different ages in different children, even in the same family and even in those who have enjoyed the same stimulus and support in their early years setting. The stages we describe are broad and should be taken as applying to children in general. They are not tests for individuals, and there will be many exceptions.

2. **There are several major areas of independence.** At any one time, a child may exhibit different stages of development in some or all of these areas – for example, in self-esteem and relationships with others (developing as an independent person); in life skills

(developing the skills of independent living, such as feeding, dressing, etc.); in learning how to learn (using experiences and the environment for learning, finding the things you need, asking for help, co-operating with others, etc.).

With these reservations in mind, we have organised our descriptions in three bands:

## Band 1: The first two years – the age of emerging independence

By about 18 months, most children have made attachments to at least one other person as well as their mother (their father, brother, sister, grandparents, childminders, and their key person in a setting, all feature here). This stage is not a deepening dependence, but a beginning of independence, the moving on from reliance on one person to interaction with a wider group, but with no lessening of attachment to their mothers.

> ...babies' brains are growing fast and the brain develops as it responds to streams of input coming from the baby's surroundings.
> *Goldschmeid & Jackson, People Under Three; Routledge; 2003*

As well as recognising a wide range of familiar individuals, the child has learned to anticipate happenings during his day, establishing a rhythm of activities and events.

Evidence of growing independence at this stage will include attempting to drink from a bottle or cup he holds himself, or holding a spoon and bringing it to his mouth. The child will help when you dress him by holding out his arms or feet. He will reach out for objects and toys, and he can occupy himself with these for a while when he wakes after a nap. He is able to play for short periods by himself, using familiar objects which he can select, handle and explore himself. He is able to walk alone for short distances, although sometimes needing to hold on to furniture or a willing hand.

If his attention is captured (for example with a treasure basket) he can concentrate for long periods on choosing objects and investigating them, and this is crucial experience in developing skills of investigation and learning how to learn.

> When presented with a treasure basket attention may last up to an hour or more.
> *Goldschmeid & Jackson, People Under Three; Routledge; 2003*

By the time a child reaches her second birthday, she has usually mastered the fundamentals of spoken language and she is experimenting with words, phrases and sentences. She has a vocabulary of

around 200 words and often learns two or three new words each day. She attaches words to objects in real life and through simple pictures in books. She is much more mobile, and may also be developing a growing independence in daytime toileting, washing and grooming and in making simple choices.

Our two year old's early assertions of her independence can sometimes look like sheer wilfulness, and this often leads to altercations with other children and with adults. Not for nothing has this stage been called 'the terrible twos'! Life seems like a never-ending series of compromises, explanations and defusion of confrontation. She is old enough to have an opinion, but has not yet developed any sense of proportion. Neither is she willing to negotiate or compromise. She has not yet learnt to delay gratification. She usually has clear ideas of what she wants, and what she wants, she wants now! As she becomes more verbal, parents and other carers swing between delight and despair – delight in her achievements and despair at her determination to have her own way! Sadly it is around this time that children often collect their first smack from an exasperated adult.

But let us look at what is going on. At this stage the child is laying down the brain pathways which will in time enable her to negotiate and see others' points of view. However, this newly found independence is not fully developed and often results in inconsistency and conflict. For example, she swings from reluctance to leave a familiar carer on one day to supreme confidence on the next. She is fast developing an awareness of herself as a separate being and of other's roles and behaviours. Simple imaginative play emerges at this stage, often with an accompanying commentary but, as with other forms of play, it is likely to be played in parallel with other children. She continues to delight in books and stories and she can grasp a crayon or brush to make marks and paintings.

The two year old asks constant questions, and will continue to do so for several years, gradually refining the questions and making better sense of the answers.

## Band 2: From about two to around four – the age of exploration

During this stage children reach half their adult height, increase their vocabulary to as many as 2,000 words and develop some fifty percent of their eventual ability to learn.

Physical independence often leads to unaided dressing, undressing, handwashing, toileting and use of a fork or spoon. When taking a drink the

*What helps a child to become an independent learner?*

child, if allowed, pours from a suitably sized jug for himself and others, passes drinks round with minimal spillage, and drinks from a cup without help.

Language development is fast at this stage, as he makes sense of the patterns of language, logically extending newly acquired words and concepts by linking them to the ones he knows, and often coming up with novel and memorable new versions. He sings, chants, hums and gives running commentaries on his activities in a non-stop torrent of words and noises. His growing command of language extends to socialising in conversations at snack and meal times, and to explaining and negotiating with adults and other children during play.

His physical skills have also improved. He can now avoid obstacles as he runs around, or rides trikes and other wheeled toys with enthusiasm and growing expertise, often shouting 'Look at me' as he goes. He climbs up and down steps with alternate feet, and negotiates ladders and other climbing apparatus with agility.

His play is now more often collaborative, particularly in role-play and small world situations. Although he is still often determined to follow his own agenda, there is an emerging willingness to take turns, to share and negotiate, and he often shows a developing sense of humour and fun.

Independent behaviour and skills emerge quickly at this stage, if encouraged and rewarded by those around him. Many children in this age band have already experienced settings outside the home, and in early years settings as well as at home, children have opportunities to master new skills and explore independence, beginning to negotiate and choose their friends and play activities. They are also ready to help with simple organisational duties, such as preparing for snack time and clearing up at the end of a session.

It is at this time that gender and racial stereotypes can influence children's behaviour. There is a frequent assumption that boys have more ideas, are more inventive, thoughtful and active than girls, and that girls are more suited to being the onlookers and followers. Practitioners should be aware of these stereotypes, and ensure that expectations for girls and boys are not different. Girls may need more encouragement and support at this

*Independent Learning in the Foundation Stage*

stage to become independent learners, rather than followers, and practitioners should make sure that positive images of diversity and creative thinking are promoted in books, pictures, games, toys and activities.

## Band 3: From four plus to about six – the age of consolidation

By the age of around four children have completed the first and most dramatic stage in laying down the necessary neural pathways in their brains. The four to six year old is refining and solidifying her responses and building on her early learning. She is now confident in looking after her personal needs, although she may still need some reminders. She can manage dressing and undressing with skill, even dealing with difficult fastenings like zips, apron ties and buckles.

Our four to six year old is able to make links between speech production and speech comprehension. She is able to understand and participate in verbal communication at a complex level. Her vocabulary is wide and varied. She delights in word and sound games and often explores books with intense concentration.

The human brain begins growing in the womb, and the majority of this development does not slow down until the age of six. Neural connections that don't develop within the child's first five years of life may never develop at all.

*Rose and Nicholl, Accelerated Learning for the 21st Century; Piatkus Books; 1998*

She negotiates with other children and adults and is able to plan at least part of her day. At this stage her attention span expands. She wants to choose her friends, her games and activities, and she will concentrate on these – alone and in a group – for increasing lengths of time. She becomes more adept at selecting resources and carrying out tasks, spending less time flitting from activity to activity. She is more involved in what she is doing, and increasingly takes the initiative.

Between five and six the spoken accent she hears around her will probably be fixed in her speech for life. This is the time for inventing rules for play and for games, for negotiating turns, for taking some risks and for making plans – taking a full share of responsibility for her actions in her class and at home, if she is encouraged to do so. At this stage, she is capable of pouring drinks, following simple recipes and rules, planning her day and recording her own activities. She can follow rules and collect and organise the things she needs for an activity, rearranging and putting things away, and she can work with other children to build, play games, play out stories, construct and create.

During this period children develop quickly and acquire many of the skills they need for later life. Given what we now know about brain development, it makes even more sense to give them an early start on the

road to independence. Every experience we offer to the children we work with must expand, not restrict their confidence. Every activity we plan must build on existing independence while giving opportunities to take this independence further. The curriculum guidance for the early years, such as the Areas of Learning and Development of the EYFS in England, gives detailed information on each stage of development and the ways in which adults can support and extend children's independence, particularly at this stage.

As we have said before, enabling independent learning is not easy. It is a road fraught with decisions, debate, flexibility and shared ownership. Practitioners need to recognise the developing skills of independence in their settings, recognise and celebrate diversity, use the curriculum guidance to help them recognise the starting points and development of individuals and groups. They also have a responsibility to help parents to understand how their children are developing, and make sure that newly appointed staff have a good knowledge of child development.

# Chapter 5:
# How adults can help and support children's independence

The previous chapter looked at how independence in young children manifests itself and the stages of development they go through in acquiring it, and the importance of understanding these. Children cannot respond to or take advantage of opportunities to develop independence unless these are offered at the appropriate stage. By planning and providing a rich array of materials and activities at suitable times, and supporting the children's thoughtful interaction with these in a variety of contexts, we can promote independence of both thought and action. This chapter looks at how we create and present the conditions in which the independent learner may grow and flourish; in other words, what we as adults need to say and do.

> What a child can do with assistance today, she will be able to do by herself tomorrow.
>
> *Lev Vygotsky, Thought and Language; MIT Press; 1998*

In *Creating Kids Who Can* (2002), Jean Robb and Hilary Letts list the pre-requisites for self direction, saying that 'Children will become self directed if they develop these characteristics:

- self reliance (relying on their own abilities)
- self belief (having their own opinions)
- self determination (making their own decisions)
- self awareness (knowing themselves and how they feel)
- self respect (having a sense of their own dignity and worth)
- self control and self-restraint (ability to exercise restraint over their feelings and emotions)
- self motivation (having their own incentive to do things)
- self assertion (putting forward their own opinions)
- self discipline (disciplining their own feelings or desires).'

We can recognise these as the characteristics of a well-adjusted and effective adult, not just an independently thinking child! This list is helpful in clarifying thinking about the skills we need as adults in promoting these dispositions in children. Of course, one of the most important factors is the way *we* model these characteristics ourselves, both in our professional and

our personal lives. If we are to fully understand ourselves we must be able to acknowledge and accept both the positive aspects of ourselves, and what may be regarded as the negative, darker sides of our personalities. Many adults find this difficult to do, and sometimes we don't make it easy for children.

For the purposes of this book, we will examine the implications of the Robb and Letts' list under six broad headings:

- self confidence and self respect (including self awareness)
- the ability to solve problems
- self motivation
- self reliance and the ability to makes one's own decisions (including self determination)
- self discipline and self control
- assertiveness

What does each of these really mean in action, and what can we do to help children develop them all?

## Self confidence and self respect (including self awareness

> Self awareness - recognising a feeling as it happens - is the keystone of emotional intelligence.
>
> Daniel Goleman, Emotional Intelligence; Bloomsbury; 1996

Self awareness is being aware of yourself as an individual, knowing who you are, understanding that you have feelings and knowing what those feelings are. We have to be aware of our feelings before we can learn to control them. Ask yourself these questions about your setting:

- Do children have opportunities to learn about feelings?
- Are the adults in the setting fully aware of the importance of helping children to recognise, name and acknowledge feelings?
- Do the adults recognise children's feelings?
- Are children given chances to think about and discuss their responses to different situations?

The very youngest children find it easy to own all of their feelings. They know exactly how they feel, what they want and what will make them happy. When they feel angry they scream and stamp, when they are hurt they cry and when they are jealous they lash out. When their wishes and desires conflict with those of others they express their displeasure vociferously and naturally.

*Independent Learning in the Foundation Stage*

It is the way in which we deal with such conflicts that can do the most damage. Our intention is to help but the effect is often far from helpful. In our efforts to teach our children sensitivity to the feelings of others, we all too often kill their awareness and sensitivity to their own feelings. If we tell children that it's not nice to be jealous, angry or resentful, they quickly learn that we consider that part of them to be unacceptable.

Consequently, the next time those feelings surface they may conceal them in order to keep our approval. Such behaviour doesn't make the jealousy go away, but it helps to convince adults that they are 'nice' children, worthy of love and respect. In short, they deny their feelings and quickly develop the ability to mask what they truly feel. Once this pattern is established it becomes habitual. For some people it is never broken. They spend an entire lifetime denying their real feelings, adopting so many masks that in the end they don't really know what they feel about anything. This makes it almost impossible for them to assert themselves and can have a devastating effect on self-awareness and the facility for self-direction. It is therefore of the utmost importance that practitioners:

> Punishment which hurts, frightens or humiliates children is unacceptable, as well as being ineffective.
>
> *Judy Miller, Never Too Young;*
> *Save the Children; 2003*

- **Understand that all feelings are real for the person who is feeling them**, and need to be acknowledged. Our feelings of anger and jealousy are as important as our feelings of love and compassion. Our 'negative' feelings are all part of what makes us human. What is important is that we acknowledge them, own them and deal with them constructively and appropriately. Children need to understand that it's okay to be angry, what is important is that the anger is expressed in an appropriate way. As part of managing anger children need to be taught the appropriate behaviours for dealing with them.

- **Assess their own staff development needs**. If we are not fully confident in this area we may need further training and support.

- **Devise programmes of activities**, collect and tell stories, work with persona dolls or puppets, that support children in understanding their own feelings and those of other people, and help them to develop a 'feelings' vocabulary.

- **Systematically acknowledge and name children's feelings** (and their own) throughout the daily routine.

- **Understand that we can acknowledge someone's feelings without having to agree with them**; acknowledgement does not equal agreement.

...like any learning within their lives, children will gain in skills and satisfaction far more effectively if adults offer plenty of encouragement with constructive and accurate feedback.

*Jennie Lindon, Too Safe for Their Own Good?; NCB Publications 2003*

Supporting the development of the children's self-awareness in this way will help them gain the emotional literacy so necessary to independence.

Self-confidence grows out of self-respect, having a sense of personal dignity and worth. Children with self-respect believe that they are equal to (but not in every way better than) other people, and this belief gives them confidence to act independently. A child who feels an all-round inferiority compared with his or her peers is much less likely to go out on a limb and exercise initiative. Believing that other children are better than they are, they will always stay in the background and wait for someone else to tell them what to do. Remember George from Chapter 1? Engaging children's co-operation without labelling them, enabling them to recognise and value themselves yet at the same time see where there are aspects of behaviour that need attention, requires good communication skills and a high degree of sensitivity. All the time and in every situation we must be aware of our own power to enhance or diminish a child's self respect.

As practitioners we are indeed powerful; the children believe us, and the labels we give them can so easily become self-fulfilling. For some children, if we tell them that they are 'naughty', 'unkind', or 'argumentative' then this may well be how they come to regard themselves, even though it is untrue, even though we can all be all of these things some of the time. Equally, what a burden it must be to be labelled 'helpful', 'kind', or 'co-operative' when we might not always feel that way. If I am labelled 'kind', I might take on this label and feel that this is what I should always be. Imagine the guilt when I fail at being a constantly kind human being! If we treat children in this way we rob them of their right to fully understand what being human is all about. This will not help them to understand their own uniqueness.

...they use praise, encouragement and comparisons to encourage children to refine their skills.

*Edwards, Gandini & Forman, The 100 Languages of Children; Ablex Publishing Corporation; 1998*

Practitioners need to value all children for who they are, not what they do, and to help them to recognise their strengths and individual personal qualities. Part of this will be the strenuous avoiding of language which might label or stereotype. Children need to be supported in developing their understanding that, although we all have different strengths and weaknesses, we are all equally important.

Practitioners need to refine their strategies for enhancing self-esteem in ways that help them to accept both their strengths and their weaknesses.

This may involve helping children to cope with potentially challenging situations without allowing them to become distressed, encouraging children to be adventurous and to welcome and involve themselves in new situations.

If children are to have a real belief in themselves there is much to consider. This is a subtle area and it is all too easy to think we are promoting children's self-esteem when what we are really doing is creating 'pseudo' self esteem – i.e. children who can only esteem themselves if they receive constant praise and approval from adults. In other words, they become reliant on our praise for their view of their own worth and are unable to esteem themselves. There are a number of things we can do to avoid this.

To begin with, it is important to use appropriate encouragement strategies. We should try not to use empty praise such as, 'I really like your picture!' 'That's brilliant!' or 'That's really lovely!' Such statements are merely personal judgements. They are non-specific and based entirely on what we think, our opinions and our preferences, giving children little insight into why we like what they have done. When we hold all the power in this way we do little to encourage children to make up their own minds and examine their own efforts. We may even try to tell the children how they have approached their work by using statements like 'You've really worked hard!'- How do we know? The child may have found the task very easy! What we have done is to make an assumption without even asking them if they think they have worked hard.

Adopting some encouragement strategies will sometimes involve us in changing the habits of a lifetime, but if we are committed to making the change we can soon adopt alternative ways of responding. For example, when children approach us with their efforts we need to make specific comments that show them that we have looked carefully at what they have achieved and thought about it: e.g. 'Look! You've painted a big house, and I can see lots of trees by the side of it and on the door you've painted a number 1.' By describing what we see we are signalling our interest in what the child has done, but at the same time leaving the power with them. They can use our comments to help them make their own judgements, with which we can either agree or disagree.

Having made specific comments and described what we see we can then move on to ask open-ended questions. We may ask, 'How did you paint this little bit here?' 'What other things could you put in your picture?' All too often we tell children what we think of what

> The important role of the adult is fostering progression in children's thinking: helping children to move forward ... through positive and interactive learning encounters between children and adults.
>
> *Robert Fisher, Teaching Children to Think;*
> *Nelson Thornes; 2005*

*How adults can help and support children's independence*

they have done before finding out what they themselves think – we must encourage children to offer their own opinions about their work. If they then say they are pleased with it, we can agree and offer our praise for their efforts. When we do this we are reinforcing their own opinions, not making up their minds for them, and of course, if they are satisfied with what they have done but we know they could have done even better, we can make suggestions, encouraging children to extend and build upon their efforts by focusing their attention on possibilities that may not have occurred to them. Or we can add additional materials or introduce new techniques or examples to stimulate their imagination and enable them to carry a project further.

> **The teacher is partner, nurturer and guide.**
> *Reggio Children; Journey into the Rights of Children; 1995*

Finally, we can involve ourselves practically in their task. When we do this we give value to what they are doing and show respect for their need to learn through practical experience and exploration. Later in this chapter we offer some help and advice on effective ways to become involved in children's play.

By making a conscious effort to engage with children in these ways we can support the development of intrinsic rather than extrinsic motivation and really help them to believe in their own ability to succeed.

## The ability to solve problems

Problem solving has been identified as one of the six key skills required for successful learning, and it is one which employers consistently put at or near the top of their lists of what they value in employees. The ability to meet the challenge of a problem, to approach it in an ordered and systematic way, to use previous experience and knowledge to develop strategies for solving it, to evaluate the success of a chosen approach, to persevere, where necessary rejecting the unsuccessful and starting again are all very sophisticated attributes. They are not, however, beyond the young child and are essential for independence of mind and thought.

> **Motivation and commitment to learning is encouraged, as children begin to understand their own potential and capabilities. Children are supported in becoming confident, competent and independent thinkers and learners.**
> *Framework for Children's Learning for 3 to 7-year-olds in Wales; Department for Children, Education, Lifelong Learning and Skills; 2008*

The UK government has suggested that there are key skills which make the most important contribution to being able to think independently and solve problems.

**Information processing skills** enable children to locate and collect relevant information, to sort, classify, sequence, compare and contrast, and to analyse relationships between the things they experience.

**Reasoning skills** enable children to give reasons for opinions and actions, to draw inferences and make deductions, to use precise language to explain what they think, and to make judgements and decisions informed by reason and/or evidence.

**Enquiry skills** enable children to ask relevant questions, pose and define problems, plan what to do and ways to research, predict outcomes and anticipate consequences, test outcomes and improve ideas.

**Creative thinking skills** enable children to generate and extend ideas, to suggest hypotheses, to apply imagination and to look for alternative, innovative outcomes.

**Evaluation skills** enable children to evaluate information, to judge the worth of what they hear, read and do, to develop criteria for judging the value of their own and others' work and ideas, and to have confidence in their own judgements.

How can practitioners in the early years create the conditions in which these skills will grow and flourish?

To begin with, we are all aware of the importance of role models for children. We know that they learn from the models we offer them of positive relationships, kind words, good manners. Models of thinking are just as important, and we must practise what we preach, demonstrating the benefits of thinking, wondering, pondering, exploring and finding out the answers to questions. We should engage children in stimulating and challenging activities and conversations which promote these skills and give opportunities to demonstrate and practise them. In the setting where such skills are valued, the adult provokes, instigates, and gives status to thinking situations, observing and following children's responses and engaging in their conversations, often recording their discussions on paper or on tape.

Next, how do we create the conditions in which children will learn to approach problems with confidence and independence of mind?

Fisher (2005) suggests that there are three main factors involved in problem solving:

**Attitude** – being interested, confident and motivated to engage with problems.

**Cognitive ability** – having the capacity to apply knowledge, use memory, think and reason.

**Experience** – being familiar with the context, materials and strategies for problem solving.

To these we would add two more:

**Opportunity** – having plenty of situations where problem solving skills can develop.

**Example** – having models of others (adults and children) who have already developed such skills and demonstrate them daily.

We need to think carefully about whether we are creating the appropriate culture for children to feel confident about solving problems, and whether we are offering a range of support mechanisms.

- Do we ask relevant questions?
- Do we remind children of similar experiences? For example, when they are thinking about ice melting in the water tray we can remind them of how their ice-lolly melted in the sun and the way the frozen puddles melted in the playground.
- Do we help them to identify existing knowledge? For example, 'Was it like the day when...?'
- Do we help children to hypothesise, to plan possible solutions and try them? For example, 'Shall we try that and see what happens?'
- Do we encourage children to reflect on the outcomes of their thinking? For example by asking them why they think something happened?
- Do we support children in tolerating uncertainty? For example, 'I don't know either, what do you think?'
- Do we give encouragement when problems are not solved immediately, helping children to generate further strategies? For example, 'Can you think of another way we could try to do this?'

## Self-motivation

**Observing and listening carefully to the voices of children will reveal insights into their learning and development that could never be captured through more formal assessment or tests.**

*Finding and Exploring Young Children's Fascinations; DCSF; 2010*

The motivation for doing something can come from many directions. Consider your own reasons for reading this book. You may have picked it up in a bookshop or library and be flicking through it out of curiosity; you may be a teacher or practitioner in training, looking for material which will help you in your future

work; you may be an experienced practitioner seeking refreshment and help in refocusing your ideas; you may be the manager or head of a setting or school in search of ways to improve the quality of your provision. If you have read this far it is presumably because you have found the earlier chapters sufficiently interesting and stimulating to make you want to go on, or perhaps you disagree so strongly with what we are saying that you are racing through in a rage to see what outrageous statements we will make next!

> All children are entitled to provision that reflects their unique characteristics, fascinations and enthusiasms. It is important to identify all children's strengths and interests at every stage in their development to ensure that this entitlement is met.
>
> *Finding and Exploring Young Children's Fascinations; DCSF; 2010*

These motivations are all different, and there are many more which we have not listed. Self motivation requires us to provide ourselves with a personal incentive (although not always a cogent reason) for doing things. At the adult level, self motivation sometimes arises from a burning interest in something, or a strong desire to carry out an action or task. Sometimes we will promise ourselves a reward for completing it, and sometimes our motivation comes from knowing that the task simply has to be done. Children need this self motivation too, although they may be more reluctant to engage in tasks simply because they need to be done!

It is important to try to understand what is involved in promoting children's self motivation. When we are fully self motivated we are usually engaged in activities that excite us, capture our imagination and through which we can experience the satisfaction of achievement. This has considerable implications for the way we work with young children – we need to know the things that motivate and interest them, and understand the influence different learning styles and preferences have on motivation.

Practitioners need to observe children closely to find out about the choices they are making and the vehicles through which they are learning most effectively. This will help to involve us in supporting children's choices and decision making, in ways that will help to develop their learning. Most children will usually learn much more effectively from the activities that they have chosen for themselves, so it is important to utilise the things that children most like to do as powerful vehicles for learning. Similarly, it is important to understand the ways in which we can teach

> Children's learning capacity is powerfully affected by the beliefs that they hold about themselves as learners, and these beliefs are in part formed by the messages we may inadvertently and unconsciously be giving them. Learning is enhanced when children feel engaged, motivated, empowered and emotionally secure.
>
> *Finding and Exploring Young Children's Fascinations; DCSF; 2010*

children the things they need to know through the choices they make; number skills can be taught outside or in the sand just as effectively as at a table, and for some children the experience will be even more fruitful.

In short, we should value and respect children's choices and decisions, and support them both in reviewing what they have done and celebrating success. For children as well as adults, the motivation to try an activity again and extend it comes from the enjoyment and success experienced the last time it was tried.

## Self reliance and the ability to makes one's own decisions

Making effective decisions requires practice; it also requires empowerment. In order to become self-determining, young children need repeated opportunities to plan and initiate their own activities. They need to be able to set goals for themselves, and these goals need to be their own, worked out in partnership with – but not imposed by – an adult. They will also need to develop the review skills and the spontaneity to adapt what they are doing on the way to achieving their goal.

Practitioners need to talk with children prior to periods of child-initiated learning to help them clarify their ideas about what they want to do. Ask the children questions about how they will achieve their goals, what materials they need and who they might work with. Early years guidance across the world promotes such child-initiated, play based activity for at least part of the day, and in some systems, such as High/Scope, practitioners plan for this type of learning to take up most of the session.

> Children are strongly motivated to play, and can experience satisfaction and deep learning in play, as they bring their current interests, questions and thinking together with strong motivation, so that they are able to function at their highest level. In play children can concentrate deeply, sustain concentration for long periods, and communicate with others to develop and maintain the play. Playful practitioners are able to engage with children in their play, and to use characteristics of play in other activities as well.
>
> *Learning Playing and Interacting; DCSF; 2009*

Of course, there may be times when the intentions and goals of the child do not coincide with those of the adult, and in such cases the adult will need to make judgements about whether to postpone their own goals and yield to those of the child, whether to reason with the child and talk them round to doing what is wanted, or whether to insist and coerce. The latter is sometimes inevitable, but hopefully it will be rare, as there is nearly always

*Independent Learning in the Foundation Stage*

room for negotiation, and the skilful practitioner will be able to handle most children in such a way that harmony prevails.

It is important to give support throughout the process of making decisions and of following them through. This will involve helping children to revise their plans where necessary and progressively enabling them to do more for themselves. Children also need to be encouraged to reflect on what they have achieved, celebrate success and identify opportunities for further development. The more we can do this, the more we will help children to work with purpose and intentionality, and the more we will facilitate the development of self-determination.

> Children are individuals and need respect. A child has the right to hold their own views and should be encouraged to do so. An adult only has the right to stop a child experimenting to progress development if it is harmful to themselves or others.
>
> *Judy Miller, Never Too Young, Save the Children; 2003*

## Self discipline and self control

Ask yourself the extent to which you help children to see the importance of self discipline to their lives. Why is it important that they should exercise their own control, rather than always being controlled? How do you support them in becoming more self disciplined?

Disciplining our own feelings or desires involves us in doing things that we don't always want to do and is an important aspect of independence. When we support children in acquiring self discipline we help them to understand that they, and not other people, are responsible for what they do and for carrying out certain obligations. This is a subtle area and one that all too often we leave to chance. However, if children are to learn self-control and self-restraint then they need our thoughtful and deliberate support. They particularly need us to be consistent and explicit.

> Keep in mind that preschoolers are still quite self-centred; they are struggling for independence and control and they think in very concrete terms.
>
> *Mary Hohmann, David P Weikart; Educating Young Children; High/Scope Press 2002*

It is helpful to identify the times of day or activities that are likely to result in conflict, either between children or between children and the management and order of the setting. Perhaps a solution might be to think of some new strategies for managing these sensitive times by finding interesting and enjoyable ways for children to be self-disciplined and to carry out their obligations. An example might be to find some music for tidying up, or trying to do it by creeping round the room as quietly as a

mouse. Children will respond well to an element of fun, and to doing routine actions in a novel and unfamiliar way. It always helps if adults model self-discipline by becoming a partner and carrying out some of the tedious tasks alongside them. Make sure you give children plenty of time, otherwise you will all be frustrated and you may end up doing the task for them instead of being a genuine partner! Also be aware that some children are adept at engaging your help in an uncongenial task and then imperceptibly withdrawing, leaving you cleaning or clearing up on your own!

An important aspect of self control is the capacity to exercise restraint over our feelings and emotions, and central to this is helping children to understand the effects of one person's actions on others.

> As children grow in their ability to anticipate and resolve social conflicts, the conflicts they must confront become increasingly complex.
>
> *Mary Hohmann, David P Weikart; Educating Young Children; High/Scope Press 2002*

Successful practitioners reflect on how they support children in this process, by helping children to understand the consequences of their own actions, in exercising control over their own actions, in helping children to generate alternative ways of doing things and in systematically teaching, modelling and reinforcing conflict resolution skills. This helps the children to understand both their own needs and the needs of others.

You can help children take control over their own actions by having clear and consistent expectations of them and encouraging them to think about the consequences of what they do. Play games and carry out activities that enhance children's listening skills, but remember that one of the most important ways in which you will influence children will be by the example you set through your own actions and behaviour.

Here are some practical things to do.

- Talk to children about the importance of listening to each other.
- Help children learn about the ways in which a good listener behaves.
- Play games and carry out activities that enhance children's listening skills.
- Talk to the children about appropriate group behaviour.
- Support children in learning appropriate group behaviours.
- Give consistent positive feedback for good listening and good group behaviour.
- Help children to think about the consequences of their own actions.
- Support children in taking responsibility for their own actions.
- Have clear and consistent expectations of children.
- Teach the process of conflict resolution.

It also helps children to have some strategies for dealing with the resolution of conflict. The following model, taken from High/Scope, may provide you with a useful starting point for approaching and teaching the resolution of conflict:

1. Approach calmly
2. Acknowledge feelings
3. Gather information
4. Restate the problem
5. Ask for solutions and choose one together
6. Be prepared to give follow-up support

There will, of course, be times when we need to address inappropriate behaviours and be critical of what children do. It is important at such times to focus on the deed and not on the doer. Try to acknowledge feelings by exploring with the child the situation that is causing problems. This simple formula will help.

**When** (describe what is happening) e.g. you shout.

**I feel** (name the feeling) e.g. I get annoyed.

**Because** (describe the consequence) e.g. other children can't hear.

**So** (state what you need) e.g. I need you to put your hand up if you have something to say.

**And** (make your expectations clear and introduce a sanction if necessary) e.g. If you continue to shout out I will have to ask you to leave the group.

Remember that survival is the most basic human drive, buried in the limbic system deep in the brain. We are all born with a predisposition to put self first, and getting a child to become more aware of the needs and wishes of others is asking them to override this root programming. That is why it is so difficult to do, and why the line between independence of mind and selfishness is so delicate. Using the prompts included in this section will help you and the children to separate the behaviour from the individual and control the former without damaging the latter.

This is a subtle area and one that all too often is left to chance. However, if children are to be helped in the difficult process of exercising self-control and self-restraint then they need our thoughtful and deliberate support. Self-control and self-restraint don't

Expectations will also influence children's actual achievement: children will live up, or down, to our expectations of them.

*Judy Miller, Never Too Young, Save the Children; 2003*

Expectations will also influence children's actual achievement: children will live up, or down, to our expectations of them.

*Judy Miller, Never Too Young, Save the Children; 2003*

just happen, they are disciplines that have to be learned, and in helping children to learn them we need to be consistent and explicit.

Working seriously on this aspect requires us to make time for the process, and this will involve us in exploring our own beliefs and attitudes. We must ask ourselves about the extent to which we feel it to be really important, and make the same commitment to fostering in children the capability to control themselves and resolve their own conflicts as we would to the development of academic skills.

## Assertiveness

In many situations our ability to act independently will depend on our ability to assert ourselves. However, it is important to be clear about what is meant by assertiveness. Assertiveness is often confused with aggression, but true assertive behaviour is never aggressive. Rather, it is a direct communication designed to tell someone exactly how we are affected by a situation, at the same time as respecting the feelings of others, and it relies on a sound and healthy concept of self. An assertive communication tells someone what we **see** (generally factual information), what we **think** (this may be an opinion or an assumption), what we **feel** and what we **need**.

It seems likely that the negotiating arrangements between adult and child are recorded in a child's brain during the second year of life. As the child grows, the pattern established will then be used whenever conflicts arise.

*Sue Finch, An Eye for an Eye Leaves Everyone Blind; Save the Children; 2003*

When our communication contains all these component parts we give a 'whole' message and leave someone in no doubt about what we are saying. Failure to do this can result in a contaminated message, leaving people to make up their own minds about what we see, think, feel or need. Usually this leads to misunderstanding, and in turn is often followed by confusion and conflict.

Practitioners and others who work with young children must be clear about what is meant by assertive communication. They need to support children in understanding how conflict arises and helping them to sort it out so that everyone feels valued and listened to. Practitioners need to see conflict as an opportunity for learning, rather than an irritating interruption in the daily routine, and a vital part of this will involve helping children to understand that community life is based on co-operation, compromise and consensus. It will also help if you can model assertive responses to

*Independent Learning in the Foundation Stage*

situations where conflict arises, and encourage children to make direct, polite interactions with each other. Although very young children may not be able to understand this model from an intellectual point of view, they internalise it very quickly when they see it consistently applied by the adults around them.

*   *   *

We have suggested above some of the things adults need to address in their interactions with children in order to help them move towards independence, and it is worthwhile giving some attention to the nature and quality of the interactions themselves. When we are involved with children in their play and in their conversations with each other, the ways in which we do this will help or hinder the development of the skills and capabilities we are trying to encourage in the children in our care.

Adult involvement in what children are doing is often referred to as intervention, and sometimes as interaction, which prompts the question, 'Is there a difference?' An exploration of the meanings behind these labels does expose some subtle distinctions.

> Collins English Dictionary defines **intervention** as 'the act of intervening ... any interference in the affairs of others'. The same defines **interaction** as 'a mutual or reciprocal action or influence.'

The two terms are distinct in emphasis and have a very different feel. Intervention is associated with interference and intrusion, and sometimes this is necessary. As practitioners, if we see two children attacking each other with scissors or using a hammer inappropriately we make a necessary and appropriate intervention! On the other hand, when children are engaged in meaningful play, the last thing we want to do is to interfere or intrude into that process. Such an intervention could well have a negative effect, destroying the play and the potential for learning. Most of us are familiar with this scenario and struggle to avoid it happening - we are eager and enthusiastic to enter the children's play, desperately wanting to 'open doors' for them and be the facilitator of deep learning. It does little for either our self esteem or their learning when they all get up and walk away!

By paying attention to a few simple principles we can master the art of sensitive intervention, and this is very important. It is

> Practitioners often have difficulties knowing when and how to interact in children's self-initiated play. They often make the mistake of going into a play activity with lots of questions, and may try to take on a role that does not flow easily into the play – one practitioner described this as 'going in with your size tens and flattening the play'.
>
> *Learning, Playing and Interacting; DCSF; 2009*

quite right that we 'interfere' in children's play to facilitate learning, but unless the initial intervention is carried out with sensitivity, meaningful interaction cannot follow. If we are truly committed to empowering children by enabling them to 'do it for themselves' we must be fully aware of the ways in which our actions might influence their play.

When we understand how much young children gain from seeing themselves as problem solvers and from experiencing the satisfaction of sorting things out for themselves we realise how important it is to get this balance right. But this is only the first step. Once we have made a commitment to involving ourselves in children's play with the conscious intention of promoting independence in learning there is still a long way to go, and unless we take time to 'tune in' to what is going on things can go badly wrong. Most early years practitioners will know what it feels like to have made an enthusiastic attempt to enter children's play, only to find that the children, resenting our interference, have all got up and moved to another part of the setting! Think about these notes made during the observation of a nursery class.

> A group of children are deeply involved in play in the home corner. Anxious to extend their play and further promote their learning the practitioner throws herself into the action.
>
> 'Can I come in?' she asks cheerily. 'I'd love a cup of tea!'
>
> She sits down and begins to ask a string of questions. While not actually ignoring her, the children make polite, but lukewarm responses, and exchange glances with one another. Undeterred, the practitioner perseveres, at first unaware that some of the children have begun to remove the furniture from the home corner and set up the play some distance away. By degrees the rest of the children begin to join them. It is some time before the practitioner realises that her presence in the home corner was nothing but an intrusion. They were simply too kind to ask her to go away, preferring instead to move the location of their play.

If children are going to become independent learners they need access to gifted adults who can intervene and interact appropriately and sensitively. Many of us already possess the gifts needed to do this well, and we initiate interactions intuitively; but by interacting more consciously and becoming more aware of what we are doing, we can become even more effective. Adopting some of the following techniques may help.

## Observe before you intervene

Next time you are about to involve yourself in children's play, make a conscious effort to spend a few minutes observing the situation before you leap in.

*Independent Learning in the Foundation Stage*

Take time to stand back and really look at what is going on. Tune in to what the children are saying. Pay attention not only to the meaning of what they are saying but to the language they are using, and observe how they are interacting with each other. Making a conscious effort to go through this process will enable you to really understand what is going on and make informed decisions about how to proceed. In fact, in some cases you may actually make the decision not to involve yourself, on the basis that such an involvement would have a negative effect on the play. It is a sensitive balance, but there are some occasions when the children will simply get on better without our involvement, where the play is so private and intimate and the children are concentrating so hard that any form of adult participation would be an intrusion. If we have taken the time to observe, such occasions are usually very obvious; but what if we are not sure? After all, we are there to facilitate children's learning. Doesn't this mean that we must get stuck in? In the event of such uncertainty consider trying the following approaches.

## Join in sensitively in parallel

Quietly sit down near the children and begin to play with some of the materials and equipment they are using. Engage in some 'self-talk', describing what you are doing, talking to yourself rather than addressing the children. This is like a child's solitary play, and it gives the children the opportunity to make clear choices. They can decide to involve you, or not. Usually within a fairly short space of time you will find the children beginning to respond to your self-talk, and starting to draw you into their play. If not, the next stage is to initiate some parallel talk. Start to comment, still to yourself, on what some of the children are doing. Copy some of their ideas and follow their lead in the play. Be careful, still, not to intrude. Watch what they are doing but avoid speaking directly to them until they speak to you.

This usually does the trick. However, any failure to respond can be taken as a clear message. If you are still talking to yourself ten minutes later you can take it as read that your involvement is not welcome! This is the cue to slip quietly away – although we have to say that in our experience this seldom happens. The point of the exercise is that it leaves the power with the children. The result is that usually they will welcome your involvement and enjoy bringing you into their world. The challenge then is about how to extend and enrich what they have started.

### Extend the play

Once accepted as a partner you are in a position to move the play on in ways that may not have been possible had you not become involved. Now is the time to extend children's thinking by making suggestions, asking open-ended questions and discussing ideas as you and the children work together.

Sounds easy, doesn't it? But what will become immediately apparent as you engage in this process is that you need to give attention to the sort of questions you are asking.

## Asking useful questions

Asking questions is one of the most frequent interactions between practitioners and children, and the questions usually go in one direction. A government survey noted that 75 per cent of the talk in classrooms was done by the teacher. Moreover, 75 per cent of that talk was questions. On average teachers asked one question every eight seconds! No wonder children sometimes feel bombarded by adult demands. However, it is not just the quantity of the questions which is significant but their quality. So many questions we ask have vague purposes and do little to extend understanding.

It is often hard to monitor this yourself, so as a colleague for some help. Pick someone you know well and trust, and ask them to monitor your interaction with a group of children for 10-15 minutes. If you can manage, say, three periods of five minutes while the children are pursuing different activities the exercise will be even more helpful. Get them to write down all the questions you ask. Afterwards you will be able to undertake a simple analysis to ascertain both the frequency and the quality of your questioning. You may prefer to carry out the same exercise by recording yourself on tape and listening to the proceedings afterwards. In either case, the aim is to collect a random sample of questions to give an insight into your questioning technique.

Consider each of the questions you asked and ask yourself whether it opened up opportunities for dialogue, or restricted them. Decide whether each was:

### A closed question

This is a question that can usually be answered in one word. e.g. 'What is the name of this shape?' Closed questions are often useful for a quick check on understanding. They do not generally require much thought by the answerer and do not generally provide much challenge.

**A thought-provoking question**

This is a question to which there is a right answer, but you have to think about it, e.g. 'When you made a cake this morning, what was the first thing that you did?'

**An open-ended question**

This is a question to which there is no single right answer, but a range of possibilities about which children will have to really think, e.g. 'We have got some string, sequins, paper, glue and a collection of cardboard boxes. What are some of the things we could do with these materials?'

You may well be surprised at the balance between these three types of questions when you come to analyse your own work, and it is not unusual for most people to ask closed questions most of the time. Did your questions really make the children think?

Here are some typical questions taken from observation of early years practitioners. What sort of questions are they? Which ones will get the child thinking?

- Are you going to play with these cars or not?
- We have got some wood, plastic and bubble wrap here. What are some of the things you could make?
- When you made that model, what was the first thing that you did?
- The glue pots keep getting knocked over. Can you think of a safer place to keep them?
- Is a carrot a fruit or a vegetable?
- What number comes before six and after four?
- Sam is upset because his friend is not there. Can you think of something that might make him feel better?
- What is your favourite story book?
- How do we know if the sun will shine this afternoon?

A disgruntled four year old was once heard to enquire, 'Why do you keep asking us questions when you already know the answers?' By asking fewer questions and ensuring that the ones we do ask are quality questions we can stimulate and challenge

The teacher's role is to ask good, open ended questions that stimulate children's thinking and provoke discussion – to facilitate, orchestrate and gently guide so that the conversation does not stray too far from the subject, so that every child has a chance to participate, and so that children consider the matter at hand with all their attention and interest.

*Louise Boyd Cadwell, Bringing Reggio Emilia Home; Teachers' College Press 1997*

*How adults can help and support children's independence*

children's thought processes and enable them to move towards greater independence in their thinking.

In the previous chapter we presented a list of the characteristics of the independent learner compiled by a group of practitioners. It is an exercise we often employ in our training, and all the lists produced are remarkably similar. Consider this one, expressed more directly in terms of behaviour and practical capabilities than the one in Chapter 4.

Independent children can and should learn:

- to recognise when it is necessary for them to go to the toilet and manage the process for themselves, including washing their hands.
- to make choices about what they would like to eat at snack time, sometimes becoming involved in the preparation of food and the tidying up and washing up of utensils, etc.
- to dress themselves, do up their own buttons, put on their own socks and fasten their own shoes. It is not appropriate to always do it for them when they are perfectly able to do it for themselves. We need to manage our own impatience and realise how children will benefit from doing things for themselves.
- to access materials for themselves, selecting what they need for a particular activity.
- to help take responsibility for the care of the physical environment.
- to contribute to the welfare of those less fortunate than themselves by being involved in a variety of projects, e.g. raising money for charity.
- to undertake a range of tasks that raise their levels of co-operative consciousness and contribute to the welfare and smooth running of their community, e.g. washing paint pots, caring for living things, putting newspaper on tables for creative activities, sweeping up sand, helping to empty water trays, planting things in the outside area.
- to play co-operatively with others, taking turns and responding to conflicts constructively and with an understanding of another's point of view.
- to review and consider what they and others have done and to form judgements about its quality and value.

We all like to have in our groups children who possess these capabilities but, as we have said, they do not always come naturally. They are the right of every child but not necessarily innate in every child. Most children need to be shown how to do these things through demonstration, example and practice. We have tried in this chapter to isolate some of the key aspects of learning independence, and to explore their implications, giving pointers to

some of the things that adults can do to help children develop the capacity to think and behave independently.

Of course, we are not the only ones who affect children's learning. We must not forget that most children spend only a small proportion of their time in our care, and that families have a far more significant and continuing contribution to make to the development of independence in their children. Discussion with parents, carers and other significant adults will be an important part of our approach, and we offer some guidance on relationships with parents in Chapter 9. However, providing the experiences we have described will go a long way towards creating the conditions in our own settings in which the independent learner can thrive. In the next chapter we look at how the physical environment can contribute to those conditions, and in Chapter 7 we look at ways of promoting independence in learning through the aspects of the curriculum.

## Summary

Adult involvement is crucial to supporting emerging independence.

We should identify the key skills of independent learning, particularly those associated with self-awareness and self-knowledge, and understand how practitioners can best support these.

We should recognise that acting positively to enable independence of mind in children often requires a substantial shift in mind-set on the part of adults.

Interaction, intervention and interference are very different things, and have different effects on children's developing skills.

# Chapter 6:
# What the setting can contribute to independent learning

Where does independence flourish? What is the best environment for its development? Are there schools or school programmes where independence is encouraged and children demonstrate all the skills we value?

A rich and varied environment supports children's learning and development. It gives them the confidence to explore and learn in secure and safe, yet challenging indoor and outdoor spaces.

*EYFS Principles into Practice cards 'The Learning Environment'; DCSF; 2008*

Consider our current obsession with house and garden 'makeovers', our continuing interest in gardening and DIY, the effort and investment that is committed to new office buildings and community spaces, and the care with which we arrange our personal spaces at work and at home. These all demonstrate our belief that the environment in which we work, play and take our leisure is of paramount importance to our sense of wellbeing, our work rate and even our health.

In this chapter, we explore the effect of the setting, the environment and the accommodation on the development of independent learners. We have looked in particular at the environment in the pre-schools and toddler groups in Reggio Emilia in northern Italy, internationally recognised as providing high quality environments that have had a significant effect on practice throughout the world. You can find out more about the Reggio approach in Chapter 8.

In their book *People Under Three*, Elinor Goldschmeid and Sonia Jackson write 'The physical environment exerts a major influence on how nursery workers feel about the job and on the quality of experiences they can offer the children'. Of course, the same must be said for children over three and the practitioners who work with them. However, many of our youngest children work and play in settings which are far from ideal. They suffer cramped conditions, low light levels, multi-purpose spaces, unsuitable equipment and furniture and little or no access to the outside. The situation is improving for some, as awareness of their needs becomes more widespread and national expectations on standards for care and education are being implemented, but the variation between the best and the worst is still unacceptably wide.

Some readers will be working in these less than perfect conditions, but there are solutions to most of these problems if we start from the assumption that the children in our care deserve the best we can provide. We know how important the environment is to how we feel, think and learn, and even in the most modest of settings we can make our intentions clear by the way we organise and allocate space and resources.

The Reggio Emilia schools describe the environment as 'the third teacher' (the adult and the child are the other two). How can we ensure that the third teacher in our settings has the best opportunity to be successful?

We will examine the following key aspects of the learning environment:

The building
The furniture
The resources and equipment
The outside space
Movement and circulation

Let's start with a practical look at two actual settings. Here are two very different descriptions.

**The Learning Environment involves both the people and the space in which children develop and learn. An appropriate physical environment is one where children feel safe, cared for and relaxed because they are in the continuous care of one, or a small number of, adults who are responsible for them (this includes a childminder's home). An appropriate physical environment offers access to an outdoor as well as an indoor space and should provide a place where children have opportunities to explore, learn and develop with the support of sensitive, knowledgeable adults.**

*Effective practice: The Learning Environment; EYFS pack; CD Rom; DCSF; 2008*

## Room 1

The door to the setting is at the end of a corridor and has a glass panel, which has been covered by notices and reminders for parents. Some of these are very out of date. They include instructions about leaving and collecting children, times for collecting part timers, addresses of suppliers of name labels, calendar dates, etc.

Inside, the room is crowded. Pictures have been displayed on the windows to prevent parents from distracting the children as they wait at the end of the day, and the lighting on this spring day is dim, despite the sun outside.

There is an abundance of furniture, which has to be negotiated by children and adults, leaving little free space for circulation. There is a very small carpet area for group times. There is no clear indication of the purposes of different areas of the room or how resources and activities are

grouped and stored. The furniture, although child sized, is old and some pieces are splintered and grubby. The low shelves for storage of materials and equipment are hidden behind curtains, which are frayed and faded, hanging unevenly from stretched wires. Where the shelves are visible, the boxes of equipment are in jumbled piles, unlabelled, often with damaged or shabby boxes.

Display boards are placed high up on the wall, often at adult height. They hold drawings attached by pins direct to the board. There are no labels or explanations. The children's lockers have peeling labels and are leaking items of work and clothing. The adult's table and chair are piled high with papers, books and children's work. Sand and water trays are new but their contents are dusty, worn and uninviting. The domestic play area contains a box of jumbled clothes, a pram with a naked doll and a disorganised collection of plastic cutlery and crockery.

The door handle to the outside play area is stiff and the door is heavy to open, with no stay to stop it slamming. Outside, the play area is bleak, with an uneven surface. Litter has blown into the corners from the street outside. The flower beds are bare and trampled, the fixed apparatus has peeling paint and rusty surfaces, and although there has been an attempt to make the area more inviting with some low benches and tubs of geraniums, the overall appearance is of neglect.

Settings like this are less common in the UK since the publication of guidelines on practice, and particularly the regular inspection regime.


## Room 2

This room is off a welcoming lobby, carpeted and with chairs for waiting parents, a vase of flowers and a small selection of photo books celebrating events in the school. The door to the room has a glass panel through which the room and the children can be clearly seen. The notice on the door says 'Welcome to our class. Today we have been making biscuits with Mrs Durber. Two of our chicks have just hatched. Come in and see them!'

Inside, the room is bright, clean and cheerful. The sun streams in through windows and the open door to the outside area. Children's work is displayed with care on low boards and cupboard tops, with labels made by the children themselves as well as explanations and accounts in children's words written by adults.

The furniture, although old, is clean and well cared for. For example, an old cupboard has had its doors removed and has been painted to provide open access for the children. Other shelves and trolleys are well organised

*Independent Learning in the Foundation Stage*

and accessible. Boxes and trays are clearly labelled with pictures and words. Colour coding helps children to put things away in the places where they go.

The painting area is inviting, with a variety of types, colours, sizes and shapes of papers, a range of brushes and clean aprons. There are labels and signs to help the children to organise their work. The incubator and a collection of books and pictures about eggs and chickens are located nearby, where they can provide a stimulus for pictures. Other areas include a carpet area for large bricks, a writing table and a book corner with bean bags where children can sit comfortably while they look at the books.

Outside, the sand and water play is in large washing-up bowls, with a small basket of high quality resources for each, carefully chosen to promote learning.

Role-play, too, is outside today. The stimulus is a trolley of equipment for window cleaning (brushes, mops, cloths and buckets, overalls and hats) as well as clipboards for bills and money for payment. In the shed are ladders and trucks for transport. These are well arranged and easy to get at. The flower beds are well tended, and climbers have been planted to provide a screen against traffic noise and wind. Chimes and ribbons hang from a tree, and there are small groups of child-sized plastic garden furniture scattered about on the grass.

## Which setting would attract you?

Imagine you are a new child, walking into your own setting, and think about the things you would see and the ways you would feel.

Almost every book on the early years stresses the impact of the environment on the quality of children's learning. Not only does it affect what they do and how they do it but the building, its surroundings and its contents have a marked effect on the way children feel, react, behave and interact.

> Children have a right to grow in places that are well maintained and pleasant, and schools can not be exempt from this responsibility.
>
> *Ceppi & Zini, Children, Spaces, Relationships; Reggio Children 1999*

When there is too much space, children's play and learning can be just as adversely affected as when there is too little. Over-bright lighting is just as difficult to cope with as dimness. Too much choice can confuse; too little choice restricts. Furniture or equipment which is too small is even more frustrating than stuff that is too big.

However, in exploring these and other issues of environment we are well aware of

> Space has in itself a calming and beneficent effect.
>
> *Susan Isaacs, The Educational Value of the Nursery School; 1954*

the restrictions facing many practitioners, and we have tried to suggest some ways in which improvements can be made, even in the most inhospitable physical settings.

We must all continue to stress that nothing is too good for the youngest children, and we must keep exploring all the avenues we can to improve what we already have. The early years Foundation Stage and the current national interest in young children is a good start, but we must not be satisfied with second best.

## The building

The building in which you and the children work exerts a powerful influence on the quality of the provision. Private and voluntary settings often have to put up with the accommodation they can get. Even within the maintained sector space, design, access and organisation vary widely.

The best purpose-built nursery classrooms and schools have convenient toilet facilities, bathrooms, kitchens, child height cupboards and door handles, accessible outside play space, friendly flooring, good natural and artificial light and plenty of space. However, in some settings, accommodation is not so inviting, pack-away settings shared with other users in community buildings, or 'emergency' spaces pressed into service for rising numbers of Reception children. It is difficult to accept this wide difference in quality, when we are attempting to provide an entitlement to quality.

**Hygiene is fundamental in a school environment. The risk to be avoided, however, is that of creating an environment that is super-cleanable, totally smooth, mono-material, dry and cold, and thus impoverished on the sensory level.**

*Ceppi & Zini, Children, Spaces, Relationships. 1999*

We must hold on to the emerging criteria for quality provision for young learners, and however difficult our individual circumstances there are likely to be, things we can do to improve them. A declaration of quality covers both inside and out, the quiet spaces, the messy, active areas, provision of storage for equipment and unfinished work, places to communicate or to be unobserved and spaces for creativity, to be other people, to reflect or to rest.

A group of architects looked at some of the most highly praised pre-schools, those in Reggio Emilia in Italy. They identified some of the key features which make the Reggio school buildings so effective, and drew up guidelines. You may not yet be in a position where your setting can meet these criteria, but it is useful to have them as something at which to aim, in part if not in whole.

*Independent Learning in the Foundation Stage*

## Transparency

Early years settings are community buildings, in many countries funded by the state, and as such they need to be visible. The building should be as transparent as possible, both from the outside and the inside. It should be visible to parents and give information about the outside to children. Windows, glass screens, doors with glass panels at child and adult height should be kept clear and free of covering, letting in natural light, the seasons and the outside world. It is very tempting to use the windows for display or to cover up the view to prevent distraction, but the message we give when we do this is that a secret activity is going on inside and that children must not be distracted by the real world outside. We should let the outside world in and encourage those outside to see what we are doing.

## Communication

Linked with transparency is the notion of communication between and within spaces. Each space in the setting should demonstrate the values and activities it promotes. The entrance and the walls, covered with the children's work, together with notices for parents, photo albums, displays of children's work, and statements about the setting itself give a clear indication of what the place is about. Tables with plants, ornaments and baskets of interesting materials offer a friendly welcome and convey the message that this is a place enjoyed by both children and adults.

> No space is unimportant, no space is marginal. Each space communicates its own personality.
>
> *Ceppi & Zini, Children, Spaces, Relationships. 1999*

Adults and children need to collaborate and communicate with each other, with parents and the community. While ensuring that there are quiet spaces and hideaways, you should also ensure that people in your setting can see each other as they work and play, through external and internal windows, doorways and screens, spaces and holes between furniture. Children also need to communicate with themselves, and mirrors are a simple way of enabling children to know themselves, become familiar with their appearance and see their expression of how they feel. How can children develop a positive self-image if they don't know what they look like?

In settings where the child's view is important, practitioners regularly bend or kneel down so they can see the setting from the child's eyes, or they go outside and come into the setting with the eyes of parents, evaluating what they can see and feel of the setting and its welcome.

*What the setting can contribute to independent learning*

## Light and shadow

Light – and its resulting shadows – is one of the most important elements of the environment. It affects our moods and our behaviour. We feel good when the light is clear, warm and helpful to the task we are doing. Lack of light has known links with depression. We need different types of light for different activities – low light for restful times, bright light for detailed work. Light that is too harsh, too dim or too diffused makes us feel irritable or ineffective. We spend too much time in the glare of fluorescent light, which makes hard shadows and can affect our sense of wellbeing. If you are working towards independent learning and calm responses, lighting should be one of your tools.

**The steel grey walls feel more suited to a factory than a school. We would love to have the walls painted a bright, warm colour instead of grey, and to have big windows so the children could see outside.**

*Wish list from a pre-school*

Daylight, and preferably sunlight, is the most important source of light for children. The colour temperature of natural light has been proved to have a beneficial effect by stimulating the pituitary gland. Windows and doors should have clear glass and be open as often as possible to allow the light and air to enter, making shadows and reflections on walls and floors, and softening the inside lighting.

Artificial light is often necessary in our climate and in some settings. Such lighting needs to be as warm and natural as possible. Consider using daylight bulbs and tubes (not the same as fluorescent tubes) to ensure the right balance of light. These may be too expensive to use everywhere, but try them at least in areas where children are going to be looking at books, painting or doing other close work. At one time energy-saving bulbs were harsh and had an eerie tinge. However, it is now possible to buy them with much warmer hues. Tungsten filament bulbs are preferable to fluorescent tubes, even though the latter might appear brighter. Fluorescent tubes flicker and this has been known to cause headaches and lower levels of tolerance, noticed by adults, but sometimes affecting children without them knowing.

Don't forget that lighting is a tool which can be used to influence moods and emotions. Encourage children to be aware of and use lighting. Sunlight and artificial light can be used to project images, make light boxes or shadow theatres - light which the children can manipulate themselves. In effective settings, the managers and practitioners check regularly to ensure that as much natural light as possible enters the rooms. If they have to use artificial light, they discuss how it could be more friendly and interesting.

*Independent Learning in the Foundation Stage*

## Colour

Children have a natural love of colour, and we assume that they will enjoy and respond to vibrant colour in all the things they see, handle and explore. However, there is NO evidence that the saturation of bright, primary colours, which is a feature of most of the equipment and toys intended for young children, is the best way to interest and stimulate them. Rather it is what adults (or manufacturers) think children ought to like.

It has been proved to be better to create a background of unobtrusive, gentle shades on walls and ceilings, which the children then 'colour' with the work they produce. Warm whites, cream and shades of blue or green give a neutral backdrop to the setting. We can then add to the palette with experiences of light and shadow, from natural and artificial sources. Individual pieces of furniture, fabrics or an accent wall can then stand out with their own character.

> The way in which children's artwork is painted on transparent sheets creates interesting layering and diffused light.
> *Abbott & Nutbrown, Experiencing Reggio Emilia; Open University Press; 2001*

When you redecorate their setting, thoughtful practitioners think of ways to use calming colours to give a sense of unity and peace.

## Floors, steps and thresholds

Floors, steps and thresholds are all important to children. Many children prefer to sit or lie on the floor to play or work; they use the spaces under tables and other furniture for hideaways and dens; they sit and stand on steps and will often pause or even set up a play situation on the threshold of a room or a space.

Flooring should, of course, always be clean but in our pursuit of hygiene we should not sacrifice comfort and texture. An ideal mixture of soft surfaces such as carpet, hard surfaces such as concrete or vinyl, and natural materials such as stone, slate, wood or cork would be wonderful! Most of us have to make do with much less, but small areas of different textures, colours and forms can make a big difference. Children can then increase their independent thinking by selecting the surface they need for the activity they are pursuing, be it building with bricks, reading, dressing up or messy work with paint or clay. The important thing is that they should have the opportunity to exercise choice.

> The environment is a living, changing system ... it indicates the way time is structured and the roles we are expected to play. It conditions how we feel, think and behave; and it dramatically affects the quality of our lives.
> *Penny Greenland, Hopping Home Backward; Jabadeo; 2000*

Where possible, steps and thresholds should be wide enough for a

static activity to continue without preventing passage between spaces. If you have double doors, open both; if you have steps inside or out, encourage colonisation. On a visit to an early years setting in the north of England one of the writers saw in the baby room a ramp between the indoor space and the outside, which the babies used freely to crawl between indoors and out. This allowed them to make independent choices about where they would be and what they would explore.

In many settings, there is discussion of how a choice of floor surfaces could be provided. Practitioners ensure that there is enough space for children to work on the floor if they want to, or use the floor spaces underneath furniture, on steps or on thresholds.

## Display and presentation

Looking at the quality and content of the displays in a setting offers one of the best ways of judging its quality. The way in which the work of children, practitioners and other adults is celebrated and shown will give a clear message to any visitor by revealing the levels of respect and independence given to the children. Where children are valued, their work is carefully presented and displayed on boards, tables and centres of interest, which provide a record of past and present projects. Teachers' transcripts of children's words carefully caption the work of each child. Adult art and artefacts are included alongside those of the children. Light flows through transparent paintings, and collage, plants and natural materials follow the passing of the seasons. Vases of flowers on shelves and in the centres of lunch tables signal a commitment to making a home-like atmosphere. Photos of children, adults and the environment are in abundance, in books and on boards.

The entrance is obvious, warm and welcoming. Clear signs help new visitors, and the need for security does not get in the way of a genuine welcome. The display in this area is also carefully chosen and set up to give pleasure as well as information. The information on the parents' notice board is regularly updated and the board is decorated with children's pictures of themselves and their families.

In situations where practitioners have to clear up every day, the best of them make the use of flexible opportunities to display what the children do. Screens, washing lines, even clothes airers and cardboard boxes are pressed into service as portable display areas.

> The environment generates a sort of psychic skin ... an energy-giving second skin made of writings, images, materials, objects and colours, which reveals the presence of the children even in their absence.
>
> Ceppi & Zini, Children, Spaces, Relationships. 1999

## Texture and senses

Settings usually provide a wide range of visual stimulation in their environment, but the other senses are often neglected. Children are not solely visual learners, so the environment in any setting should appeal to and stimulate all the senses. Objects to touch and handle, smell or taste and which make interesting sounds are just as important as display boards with colourful pictures.

We can easily add texture and form by leaving some walls natural as brick or plaster, mounting tiles and objects on surfaces or stripping furniture so the grain of the wood can be felt. Baskets and displays of natural materials such as cones, leaves, shells and flowers can be touched, handled and smelt. Displays can include three-dimensional objects, textures, scents, sounds and flavours. Aromatic oils and perfumes, perfumed plants, non-caustic and non-toxic cleaning products such as 'green' polishes, the smell of lunches cooking, baking and snacks will all stimulate the sense of smell.

> In order to grow and learn, the human brain needs to be stimulated by sensory experiences which take place within a rich and varied environment. In the first months and years of life, a child needs to see, touch, hear, taste and smell.
>
> *Vea Vecchi, Reggio Schools*

Within the constant 'soundscape' of children and adults working we can offer quiet areas for rest or contemplation by using screens, partitions and curtains. Carpet or acoustic matting can help to control noise. A blanket can be pinned across a corner to deaden the sound from the rest of the room and create a quieter space. We can add wind chimes, bells and rain boards inside and out to bring the sounds of the seasons and weather indoors. We can offer tapes and headphones to ensure attention and cut out noise.

# The outside

In the early years Foundation Stage the outside environment is not only important, it is a vital part of children's entitlement. Staff and children in settings where there is no safe outside place to play feel very much deprived, and rightly say they are unable to fully implement the Foundation Curriculum.

> A school should be a place that 'senses' what is happening outside – from weather to seasonal changes, from time of day to the rhythms of the town.
>
> *Ceppi & Zini, Children, Spaces, Relationships. 1999*

As with other aspects dealt with in this book, we try to balance sympathy with those who have difficulties in trying to establish what is desirable. The inside of the building

and the outside are inextricably linked. Even if your only outside space is a car park or a small patch of scrub, it has possibilities. The following section will, we hope, give you some way of setting priorities for improving what you have now.

Essential features described in the Italian research work *Children, Spaces, Relationships - metaproject for an environment for young children* (Ceppy and Zini, 1995) are:

**The entrance** This is the public area for visitors and families at the beginning and end of the day. It is the first experience given to someone entering the setting, and must give a strong message about the purposes and processes within. The path, gate, security systems, the door with its notices and views into the building - all give an initial impression which can imply an open or a closed place, transparency or opacity. The first impression for children and all visitors will be a lasting one, so make sure it is positive!

**The filter places** This is where the inside and the outside meet. Porches, steps, verandas, canopies and thresholds all seem important to children, and many choose to base themselves in these places which are neither inside nor outside. In these areas, children collect in ones and twos, often bringing things from inside to play on the threshold, obviously enjoying the light and air but not wishing to venture fully outside or needing to be involved in what is happening outside. It is a good idea to make as much of this sort of space available as you can. Open double doors, encourage children to colonise steps and covered ways as extensions of the inside. There is nothing you can do indoors that you cannot also do outdoors.

> Outside play and the environment in general, including the large trees that overlooked the play area, were (valued) by the majority of the children.
>
> *Clark and Moss, Listening to Young Children; NCB; 2001*

**The equipped and landscaped areas** Grass, static equipment and hard surfaces for wheeled toys all need careful thought as you develop them. If you have a large variety of spaces and large numbers of children you will need to plan carefully if you are to avoid accidents and territorial conflict.

Because of our climate the hard area will need to be bigger than the grass. Any static apparatus should be carefully chosen and sited. It should also be as flexible as possible; an outside area should not look like a pub garden! It is a learning environment, not one created solely for recreation. Children asked about preferences for fixed or more

flexible climbing apparatus gave a clear reply. They all opted for the flexibility of ropes, planks, tyres and mats, which they could manipulate themselves, using their imagination for ideas.

**Areas for wheeled toys and games** might be gently sloping to encourage the run off of rainwater, and can be defined by the use of permanent or temporary markings. Temporary marking using chalk will enable flexibility and encourage experiment – two keys to independent thinking.

Role-play settings, quiet areas for reading and thinking, natural and wild areas, trees and bushes all offer tranquility and can be provided even in relatively small spaces. The nursery garden has been a traditional element of early years education for almost two centuries. Reinstating this aspect of the outside is long overdue. Play in mud, sand and gravel and the production of plants, flowers, fruit and vegetables give children an excellent opportunity to see the cycle of life and to watch insects and other wildlife. The production of things children can eat is an added bonus. The garden also provides a tranquil place for stories, music, observing the seasons and the weather.

Installations for sound, light, weather and watching wildlife all have a place in the garden. So does the erection of sculptures, structures, mobiles, mirrors and pictures. In some settings all the available space is covered – a conservatory, a courtyard, a hall or play space. Even where access to the outside is not easy there are opportunities for the imaginative practitioner to use decoration, ventilation and light to give a feeling of outdoors.

A recommendation to all settings is to audit their own provision, listing all areas which could be used for any of the purposes above. They can then construct an action plan for fully exploiting and making the best use of the outdoor spaces available to them. The spaces, the building, the outside area, the light and the stimulation of the senses are all parts

Play underpins all development and learning for young children. Most children play spontaneously, although some may need adult support, and it is through play that they develop intellectually, creatively, physically, socially and emotionally.

Providing well-planned experiences based on children's spontaneous play, both indoors and outdoors, is an important way in which practitioners support young children to learn with enjoyment and challenge. In playing, children behave in different ways: sometimes their play will be responsive or boisterous, sometimes they may describe and discuss what they are doing, sometimes they will be quiet and reflective as they play.

*QCA, Practitioner Guidance for the Early Years Foundation Stage; DCSF; 2008*

of the provided environment, controlled mostly by adults, and often affected by circumstances beyond our control. The use by children and adults of these spaces and the equipment and resources they contain are things over which we all have control.

## Movement and circulation

We can't do much about the buildings in which we have to work, other than see that they are clean, safe and well decorated. But how we define the spaces inside them and encourage flow within them is within our control, and we have the opportunity to involve the children in this enjoyable activity.

Certain areas of both the inside and outside environment need to be allocated to particular activities. Sand, water and paint need a sweepable, waterproof floor; book and quiet areas need carpet and cushions; music, wheeled toys, woodwork, role-play and gardening all have special requirements, and children need to know the boundaries and rules. However, the location of these areas does not need to be fixed for life, and those settings where packing up is a daily occurrence may have the flexibility to rearrange the location of activities more frequently than practitioners in more permanent situations. The key to this flexibility is to watch what the children do and how they use the spaces they have, and involve them in discussion of what you see.

> 'A rich and varied environment supports children's learning and development. It gives them the confidence to explore and learn in secure and safe, yet challenging, indoor and outdoor spaces'
>
> *Statutory Framework for the EYFS; DCSF; 2008*

Of course there is need for a balance between constant change and stagnant security. If they are to become independent, children need to know where to find things and put them away. This implies some stability, at least in some parts of the space. If the room is to meet the needs of the children, you (and they) will be making changes as a result of experiencing and observing how they use spaces and resources, and the need for development in their play. Some children are disturbed by changes in the environment, but these are few. The majority will enjoy new arrangements and ideas, particularly if they are involved in talking about them beforehand and in the move itself.

If we are going to give children the option of changing their own environment, they will need some help. Light, portable partitions and furniture (wheeled if possible), boxes and baskets with handles, fabric in

varying sizes and colours, cones and benches all help children to be creative and make the moving more purposeful. Furniture which serves several purposes is always useful. A screen with a window can become a castle, a shop or a puppet show; a simple piece of fabric can become a tent, a picnic rug or a partition; a portable mirror can be a shop prop, a dressing up aid or, placed on the floor, the start of a whole new way of looking at things.

How flexible are you in setting up your spaces? Do the children have any ownership of the organisation of the space they work in?

> The piazza is a place of meeting, a public place of the school, which plays the same role in the school building as the piazza does in the town.
>
> *Marianne Valentine, The Reggio Emilia Approach; Scottish Consultative Council on the Curriculum; 1999*

## Resources and equipment

Look back at the examples at the beginning of this chapter. In both settings the furniture, the resources and access to them were keys to defining the quality of the experiences available to the children.

### Furniture

Furniture must be of good quality and the right size. Some settings are located in shared or borrowed spaces and have to make do with adult-sized furniture, but although this is not ideal, it is not necessarily too much of a disadvantage. The way furniture is used can be more important than its size, and some children would rather stand at a table than sit on a chair, some favour cushions or bean bags, and some seem to concentrate best if they lie on the floor. Some activities may need full sized chairs (for example while using a computer trolley or exploring the books in a library), and most children are used to coping with adult-sized furniture in their homes.

Many practitioners find that settees, armchairs and other full-sized furniture make their setting more like home and so more comfortable, so those who work in the voluntary sector, operating in church or village halls and rooms in colleges or adult centres should not get over anxious about the size of the furniture. However, the safety of the children means that you will need to keep a close eye on its condition, and that damaged furniture be

> Provide equipment and resources that are sufficient, challenging and interesting and that can be used in a variety of ways, or to support specific skills.
>
> *Guidance for the EYFS; DCSF; 2008*

removed from use as quickly as possible. A bonus of taking a more relaxed view is that once we accept that adult furniture has a use we are able to accept gifts of used but serviceable items from parents and friends.

When considering the furniture available to your setting, ask these questions:

### Relative size
Are the tables and chairs related to each other in size and height? Can children work comfortably at the table, using the chairs we have? Can children reach the shelves and cupboard doors of the storage to which we want them to have access?

### Condition and quality
Is the furniture safe and stable? Is it free from splinters on tables and chairs or chips from the paint? Does the furniture need renovating or replacing? Are catches, handles and locks safe and easy to use?

### Flexibility
Is the furniture portable? Can we, and the children, use it flexibly to change the environment? Can we move the pieces to make screens and dividers? Is it easy and safe to move, encouraging independence and innovation?

### Quantity
Is there enough furniture? Is there too much? How do we decide what is enough? What do you do with spare or unsuitable furniture?

### Type
Do we ever use full size furniture, or would we like to? Where could we use this?

## Storage
We need more storage! How often do managers in early years settings hear this cry? But often many of our cupboards and shelves could be described as the 'attics' of the early years, stacked with things that 'might come in useful one day', filling space with things we can't bear to throw away, and often resulting in poor storage and access, or shelves so full that children take their lives in their hands if they attempt to get things for themselves. This book is about independent learning. Children cannot become independent learners if they can't see, select and access their own equipment and

resources. In a setting where independence is valued the storage solutions should meet these criteria:

### Access

Can children get their own things easily? Can they see what they want? It is now evident that children need to see things to switch on the desire to work with them. Are resources in small enough containers for children to manage themselves?

### Organisation

Are things clearly grouped and labelled so children can find them and put them away again? Do you include pictures AND writing in your labelling?

### Presentation

Are things carefully and attractively stored, preferably in transparent containers, so children can see what is on offer?

### Condition

Are things checked for missing pieces, cleanliness, broken boxes?

### Manageability

Are things in manageable containers which children can lift? Have they got handles? Are big sets broken into several containers for ease of carrying?

### Location

Are things located near the play base where they are likely to be used (e.g. sand toy selections near the sand tray, collage materials near the sticking table)? Are the things they need spread out around the setting to enable access and avoid congestion?

Of course, furniture and storage are not the only aspects of resource management. Good management will not in itself turn poor quality, unsuitable and shabby resources into high quality learning experiences. Practitioners need to look further when checking their resources. They should check, monitor and constantly seek to improve:

### Condition

Are the resources in the best possible condition? If you have to buy second hand, or cope with heavy wear and tear, do you refurbish and

*What the setting can contribute to independent learning*

repair shabby furniture and resources? Do you have a policy and a budget for replacement of equipment that is worn out?

### Quality
Are the resources of the highest possible quality that you can afford? Are you insistent on the best for the children? Do you discard resources and equipment which are of poor quality? Do you shop for quality as well as price? Cheap and cheerful is not always the best value for money.

### Suitability
Are the resources suitable for the purpose and the children? Do they match your curriculum purposes in terms of the tool for the job? Do the scissors actually cut fabric, are plastic tools really best for digging? Do the resources match the range of needs of the children? Are the puzzles too easy? Is the construction set too small for their fingers?

### Flexibility
Are the resources flexible in use, or do they only suit one purpose? Can the small world people actually fit in the doll's house? Do the cars fit the road mat as well as the garage? Can resources be mixed and matched to provide new activities and games thought up by the children?

### Sufficiency
Is there enough of everything – scissors, wheels for the Lego, dressing up clothes for boys as well as girls?

### Range
Do you have a good range of equipment for both boys and girls, to reflect diversity, to meet special needs? Is the range wide enough to prevent gender stereotyping? Do you provide natural and artificial surfaces and textures, to suit both the active learner and the reflective child?

And practitioners need storage too! This should be acknowledged by their managers and by the children. Materials in preparation, records and planning sheets, items which need to be restricted from child access for reasons of safety, as well as personal property, all need to be accommodated. A cupboard, drawers or shelves which are 'off limits' to children should be a right for adults.

If you wish to promote independence in your setting, the questions can be used as the basis for establishing the children's right of access to

materials and equipment which encourage them to manage their own learning. The systems you establish should give children choice, recognise a range of needs, enable creative thinking and support autonomy. However, being independent is not about children having access to everything and being able to do anything they like. The rules must be clear, too. If they are not, children will see choice not as something which frees and enables them but as a trap inviting them to make mistakes.

# Section 3

## Promoting Independent Learning

# Chapter 7:
# How to improve provision to encourage independent learning

- What can parents and practitioners do at the early stages of learning to help children to become more independent?
- What are the essential skills and attributes that support independent learning?
- Where does independence flourish? What is the best environment for its development?
- Is independence something we can affect – something we can identify and provide for?

As we look at the setting where independence is fostered and promoted, we will see that there are plenty of opportunities to develop independence and initiative in all the aspects of learning. In this chapter, we take a range of aspects and explore how we can use them to help children to play a greater part in decisions which affect their learning – what to do, how to do it, how to work with others to solve problems. We emphasise the importance of encouraging and allowing children to be responsible for managing themselves and their activities. We concentrate on the aspects of learning rather than the areas of learning and experience, so that our ideas and advice can be more directly related to the day-to-day life of your setting. Opportunities to develop independence and autonomy are present throughout the day and in all activities; they are part of the ethos of your setting and need your consideration as you plan how you address the early years curriculum.

There are a number of factors that work against encouraging independence in children – in any setting. An organisation, even a small one, needs systems, processes and rules which make for smooth, safe and efficient operation. They are attributes of an orderly society. However, some of these will inevitably impinge on the scope of the individual to do exactly

*Independent Learning in the Foundation Stage*

as he or she likes. It is very easy to use conditions we have had imposed on us, or rules we have created for ourselves as reasons for not giving children the freedom to decide and act.

Developing independence requires time. Choosing, experimenting, exploring options, thinking and talking about possibilities all need to be allowed the space to develop. It is easy to become impatient when children take a long time to do things. How often have we all said or thought, "It's quicker to do it myself than leave it to the children." Sometimes it seems as though they are being deliberately slow, and perhaps sometimes they are, although in our experience this is rare. Under pressure to get things done, to beat the clock and to meet our (sometimes self-imposed) schedules it is tempting to do things ourselves and not wait for the children. However, we should never forget that time is one of our most important resources, and we need to ensure that children are well provided with it.

The previous chapter looked at the physical setting and considered space and access. We are well aware of the variability of accommodation, of the difficult conditions some voluntary and private providers have to endure, and of the way in which Reception and Nursery classes in some schools are banished to the least attractive and convenient spaces. And of course, all settings are short of money. However, we should not use inadequacies in the environment and resources to justify not doing what we know should be done. With imagination, problems can sometimes be turned into opportunities. And even when they can't, there is much that can be done within even the most basic setting to promote independence.

It is not always the tangibles that discourage some practitioners. There are genuine concerns about what encouraging children to be independent will mean. Will independence mean constant confrontation and conflict with children? How can I be sure children won't take inappropriate risks? Will independence be a threat to my position as an adult? What about my need to be needed? These are all natural and fair questions, and we will try to answer them.

The first step is to identify the things in your own setting which prevent you from loosening the reins, surrendering some of your control, being willing to adapt or abandon careful plans and allow the children to take the lead in deciding where the curriculum should go. Sometimes it may be necessary to persuade colleagues of the value of a different approach, changing not just minds but hearts, because this is the way to change practice. It will help if you make a conscious effort to recognise the needs of young independent learners.

In order to become independent learners, Judy Miller (Never Too Young) says, children need:

opportunity – to try things for themselves.

experience – of practising independence from an early age.

role models – of adults and other children. What we do has far more influence than what we say.

expectations – that they can and will become independent learners, given time and opportunity.

motivation – created by rewarding and praising effort and success.

information – to empower them to make choices and decisions.

With this list in mind, we shall in the following chapters explore some of the key aspects of learning:

- Role-play
- Outdoor play
- Construction
- Storytelling
- Writing
- Music, movement and dance
- Creativity and critical thinking
- Messy activities

In the chapters which follow we discuss each aspect in turn and present some ideas and suggestions for approaches and activities that will encourage children to be independent. We show links to the Early Learning Goals, offer guidance to enable you to check on the quality in your setting, and provide for each a case study which shows children demonstrating the attitudes and qualities we are seeking. We address early years practitioners directly and include guidance on things which can be done to empower children and give them ownership. At the end of the chapter we look briefly at the ways in which planning, recording achievement, display and other fundamental aspects of organisation can support the independent learner.

In each of the aspects we suggest resources and activities, and ideas for involving the children. We give particular attention to getting started, and because we believe that talking is one of the keys to thinking and learning, we provide pointers to stimulate the children to unlock their ideas through discussion.

# Chapter 8:
# Imaginative and role-play

Role-play is a vital part of children's education in the Foundation Stage and beyond. It forms the basis for story telling, writing and social development. It gives opportunities for children to play out the events they observe and experience. It provides experience of real-life situations in which they can practise their learning in maths, language and communication. It develops their creativity. And above all it's fun!

There are three major types of role-play:

**domestic play** – where the home and family are at the centre, with jobs to do and food to prepare. These domestic situations can be familiar or new. We should aim for a variety, some rooted in the children's own experience, some encouraging flights of fancy. You could try a barbecue or a country cottage, a caravan or a lighthouse, a giant's house or a palace. Remember the opportunities outside your room as well as those within it.

**transactional play** – where goods, services and advice are exchanged for money. These are endlessly fascinating to children, probably because transactions are a major part of what they observe of adult behaviour. You can include shops, travel agents, vets, clinics, markets, garden centres and many others.

**imagined worlds** – those places where stories dwell, or places the children are unlikely to visit, such as the moon or under the sea, in a pond, a cave, the North Pole, a jungle. For city children it may be the seaside, for country children it may be a tower block. Some children may have travelled several times by air but never been on a bus. To some the dark is familiar, to others it is the unknown. Give all children the chance to come to terms with the unfamiliar by exploring it through role-play.

All three types of play can be provided in a variety of ways: through 'whole body' play with access to dressing up and life sized

> Children's creativity must be extended by the provision of support for their curiosity, exploration and play. They must be provided with opportunities to explore and share their thoughts, ideas and feelings, for example, through a variety of art, music, movement, dance, imaginative and role-play activities, mathematics, and design and technology.
>
> *EYFS Statutory Framework; DCSF; May 2008*

equipment, through small world play using Lego, Playmobil, etc. and through the use of puppets, dolls or figures. A play setting outside could link with a domestic setting inside: for instance, outside there could be a train or bus, inside there could be, for example, a clinic or shop to take the baby to.

If you can offer more than one of these types of play at the same time which of these will be deeper, more complex, more intense and will offer the children richer experiences? What is the point of having a house if you can't go out anywhere? What is the point of having a shop if you can't take the food home to cook?

## Links with key Early Learning Goals:

*Communication, Language and literacy*
- Interact with others, negotiating plans and taking turns in conversation
- Listen and respond to stories and songs
- Extend vocabulary
- Use language to imagine and recreate roles and experiences, organise, sequence and clarify thinking, ideas, feelings and events

*Creative development*
- Use their imagination in imaginative and role-play and stories

Imaginative play and role-play offer children endless opportunities to develop the skills of independent learning. Imaginative children will enjoy solitary role-play sometimes, but social interaction, taking turns and sharing are vital for the success of this type of play, which makes it less easy than most activities to play on your own. Role-play gives the chance to explore first hand the roles of adults in the real world (doctors, firemen, nurses, teachers, hairdressers, mums and dads). A range of cultures and contexts can also be offered as situations for role-play, opening the door to the lives and lifestyles of the families in the local area by using implements, wearing clothes, eating food of other cultures and countries.

To experience stories in action (giants, bears, divers, astronauts) in imagined worlds provides a springboard to stories and poems. How can a child write an adventure story if he or she has never had an adventure? How can a child describe how a fictional character feels unless he or she has practised and experimented with those feelings in role?

Life skills such as using the phone, making meals, shopping and taking care of others can be practised 'in role' without anxiety or threat. Writing in role when making lists, labels, notes, letters and appointments or taking names gives practice for emergent writing and helps to reinforce both the functions and the importance of writing. Counting, checking, selling and

*Independent Learning in the Foundation Stage*

buying give opportunities to become aware of numbers and their uses; negotiating and compromising provide practice in social skills.

Role-play allows children to shape their own learning environment by contributing to, planning and providing role-play situations. We should recognise this, and demonstrate our interest in their opinions by giving them real choices and handing over some of the ownership to them.

Role-play is such a powerful learning tool, we should never neglect its impact. The domestic play area must never decline into:

- a jumbled box of assorted women's cast offs as dressing up clothes
- an assortment of old plastic plates and cups
- some battered furniture
- a couple of naked dolls in a cot with no bedclothes.

when with a little care it could have:

- simple matching picnic sets
- baby clothes which fit the dolls and simple baby bedding
- a rack or hooks for dressing up clothes with something for the boys to wear
- newly painted furniture and some new curtains.

## Getting started with independence in role-play

- Brainstorm role-play following a story or other stimulus, or at the beginning of a new topic.
- Use walks and visits to discuss what people do, jobs, shops and services.
- Invite visitors (the health visitor, dentist, parents, etc.) to talk about their jobs.
- Collect books and leaflets about jobs.
- Use items of clothing, hats and objects to start conversations about characters.
- Use video clips, photos, posters and magazine articles, as starting points.
- Start a collection of stories to stimulate role-play. Add simple props or make prop boxes.
- Use puppets to begin stories and trigger interests.
- Encourage parents to get involved by donating resources or providing role-play experiences at home.
- Try two linked role-play areas in your setting, such as:
  - a house and a food shop
  - a house with a baby and a baby clinic
  - a cave and a giant's castle
  - a garage and a car wash

- a hairdresser's and a wedding
- a garden centre and a café
- an office and a train
- a fish and chip shop and a house
- an aeroplane and a travel agent

... or expand your role play out of doors by setting up:

- a sports centre
- picnics
- painting the school (or a house)
- a barbecue
- a submarine
- a market

## Ideas for resources to support independence in role-play

- Boxes and cartons of wood plastic, cardboard.
- Planks and pieces of plywood.
- Pop-up tents and den making equipment such as canes, clips and fabrics.
- Shower curtains or sheets for spraying and painting.
- Camping equipment such as enamel mugs and saucepans.
- Collections of natural materials such as cones, nuts, stones, twigs and small logs.
- Heavy items to shift and lift – logs, stones and bricks.
- Barrows, carts and trucks.
- Lightweight furniture and screens. Baskets, mats and blankets for picnics, with matching plates and cutlery.
- Baskets, prop boxes, collections, items on different themes, from different ethnic and social backgrounds. These can be used in rotation to link with topics or activities, or children can decide who they want to be today.
- Well organised hanging space for clothes – hooks and loops on garments.
- A small bench and a safety mirror near a dressing up area. Unisex, all-purpose tabards or overalls. Hats and headbands, stickers and badges.
- Magazines, newspapers, leaflets and forms. Telephones (including mobiles) the more you have, the more they will talk. Computer keyboards and cameras
- Light fabrics that can be tied to furniture, trees, equipment to make tents and shelters, or to tie round heads or bodies.
- A tray or trolley with clipboards, notebooks and pens, white boards, blackboards, pens and chalk. Materials for making signs, notices, badges.
- Playground chalk for markings. Flags, streamers, shop signs and banners.
- Plastic cones, crates and guttering for structures. Lightweight containers,

trolleys, baskets and bags. Post boxes, road signs, traffic lights and steering wheels.

- Look out for sales and special offers. If the children can be taken along to choose the furniture and experience the shopping it will provide another opportunity for learning.
- Hats and caps for drivers and riders. Bags and backpacks.

## Managing storage and access

- Wicker baskets, and boxes with handles for props, picnics, role-play clothes
- Laundry baskets for bricks and small world play (make sure they are light enough for the children to carry)
- Hooks and shelves in your shed, so things can be hung up, and painted outlines of the objects so that the children can put them back in the right places. Cheap cotton or plastic carriers make storage easier.
- Small trolleys or stacking vegetable baskets keep items like balls and bean bags safe (also useful for outside collage, paint, sand toys, science, garden tools)
- Child-sized supermarket trolleys, bags and baskets are good for clearing up; have several so that everyone can help

## A case study of encouraging independence in role-play

In settings where the staff and children are used to working and planning together, children are involved in decisions about the setting up, location, focus, equipment, the time for change as well as the play itself. Here is a description of a Reception class where children are accustomed to being fully involved in planning what they do.

Mrs Senga, who helps in the classroom, came to school with a new hairstyle. The children were fascinated by her curls and followed her everywhere, intrigued by the new look. Mrs Senga and some of the children went to the school library to look for a book about hairdressing, but they couldn't find one. At group time, Mrs Senga was asked to describe what had happened at the hairdressers. The children asked some very complex questions, and Mrs Brennigan, their teacher, decided that a visit was indicated and on her way home she called at a local hairdresser to ask if they would be willing to cope with a couple of visits from interested groups of children.

A few days later the first group of children walked along the road to visit. The children had already had opportunities to talk about the hairdresser, so they had some ideas of what they wanted to see and ask. The obliging hairdresser had arranged to do a free cut and blow-dry for a regular customer as a focus of interest for the visit. The children watched this process intently, taking careful note of how the brushes, rollers and drier were used.

Some children made picture lists on clipboards. Mrs Senga had brought the camera and some of the children took photos. The hairdresser gave them each a little sample of shampoo to take home. He also gave them a big bag of rollers, brushes, empty shampoo bottles, some shoulder capes and an appointment book.

Over the next few days, the children brought things from home to complete the preparations – magazines, an old hairdryer (with the plug removed), a mobile phone (with the battery pack removed), empty hairspray and shampoo bottles. They also collected bowls, towels, pens and paper, purses and money. They made a price list, which included children's haircuts for the dolls. They put up posters and made a style book of pictures from magazines.

The photos from the visit were printed and mounted, including a whole series of the process of a 'wash and blow-dry' from the first visit. This really helped with sequencing an unfamiliar event. Chairs, tables, overalls and a booking desk, complete with phone, and the appointment book completed the preparations. The children decided to call their shop 'Hair Do', and with Mrs Senga's help made a big sign to go on the door.

The boys were just as keen to be involved as the girls, both as hairdressers and as clients. Visitors brought dolls from the home play area, members of staff were invited to make appointments, and parents called in to see what was going on. The children took photos of their 'salon' to send with letters of thanks for their visits.

Every child in the class became involved in this activity, and staff observed that even the most withdrawn children took part, growing in confidence as they did so. The children often adopted their parents' names when they made appointments. Their technical language and the language of transactional situations became very sophisticated, and this affected other activities in the classroom. The concentrated play lasted for several weeks, until a spell of really fine weather stimulated interest in the school garden and the children decided to dismantle the hairdresser's and use the equipment to set up a garden centre outside.

This is an example of role-play of a very high quality. The practitioners followed the interests of the children and responded positively to the leads which they gave. They watched and listened, were sensitive to the things children were interested in, and offered resources to support them. They used these starting points to extend children's learning through first hand experiences, play and talk. This in turn stimulated the imagination and creativity of the children, and gave them wonderful opportunities to develop the skills of independent learning.

It is obvious from this description that both the children and the practitioners were used to working in that way.

## Suggestions for giving your children ownership of role-play activities.

- Sometimes start your sessions by saying, 'Where shall we put the house today?'

- Set up a minimal shop, office or other setting and wait for the children to ask for additional things.
- Put up a sign, picture or label to suggest role-play ('WINDOW CLEANER', 'GARAGE', 'CAVE') then ask the children what they need to make the place work.
- Put a prop basket or box of items on the carpet or outside (cloths and brushes for a car wash, a doctor's kit and white coat, a trowel, fork and some seed packets).
- When children lose interest in a play area, ask them what you should do. Follow their lead.
- Discuss purchases of new equipment, let them look at catalogues and books to choose items. When you set up a new area or topic, make a list with them and take them shopping.
- After a visit, discuss how they can help to set up the new situation, where it should be, what it should contain.
- Observe and note the conversations going on in the role-play areas. Use these as starting points for discussions, new resources and changes.
- Pick up hints from your observations of children's interests and their self-initiated play.

## Questions to ask when you review the quality of role-play in your setting:

- How much independence do you allow your children in role-play?
- Do you encourage them to change and adapt the role-play areas, furniture, equipment, etc.? Could you involve the children more in setting up new areas? Do you encourage parents and children to contribute ideas, experiences and resources for role-play?
- Are the resources of the highest quality you can afford? Do these reflect the groups and communities living in the area and the backgrounds of the children in your setting? Do they offer opportunities for children to broaden their experience?
- Do you change the role-play areas often enough?
- Have you considered the benefits of having more than one role-play area? Is role-play on offer outdoors as well as inside your setting? Are there opportunities for informal and spontaneous role-play as well as for play in more permanent settings?
- Do you provide clothing and resources for role-play which are likely to appeal to both genders? Do you encourage children away from gender stereotyping in their play? Is there equivalence between the genders in both indoor and outdoor play?

# Chapter 9:
# Outdoor play

Outside play is an entitlement for all children in the Foundation Stage. Nowadays, parental anxiety about children's safety and the increasingly sedentary nature of home life means that children may grow up with little opportunity to play outdoors, and many have no contact with their friends at the end of the day or at weekends. Playing in the garden or the park is unfamiliar to many, and extended periods of uninterrupted physical activity are rare, even inside many settings.

It is now very evident that children who have access to the outdoor environment and natural materials every day will thrive in a way that those who stay indoors all day cannot. Outdoor provision should ideally be in a 'free-flow' system where children can move freely between the indoors and outdoors as they play, selecting and collecting their own play resources, companions and spaces to play.

Of course, some settings do not have the luxury of an on-site garden, and in these situations, practitioners need to take advantage of daily visits to local parks and other open spaces where children can run, make noise and be physically active. Taking equipment on these daily visits may mean that practitioners need to think about:

- Safe routes to play spaces
- Suitability of the play equipment provided and how to transport equipment from the setting
- Clothing for inclement weather
- Supervision in spaces that may not be enclosed
- Provision of toilets and other shelter
- Staffing

These are all reasons for NOT going, but the EYFS states that:

Being outdoors has a positive impact on children's sense of well-being and helps all aspects of children's development.

Being outdoors offers opportunities for doing things in different ways and on different scales than when indoors.

It gives children first-hand contact with weather, seasons and the natural world.

Outdoor environments offer children freedom to explore, use their senses, and be physically active and exuberant.

*EYFS Practitioner Guidance (card 3.3); DCSF; May 2008*

For those practitioners who are fortunate to have on-site play areas, there are still some issues to contend with – not least (as Margaret Edgington says) that 'there is no such thing as unsuitable weather, only unwilling adults!' Everyone needs to think about:

- Outdoor clothing
- Access and supervision
- Storage of equipment
- The effects of the weather on equipment and surfaces
- Getting out and putting away resources and toys
- Space for boisterous play while ensuring that children who need quiet can find it

In all settings the balance between risk and safety, safety and danger need to be managed. Outdoor play, on the whole, has more risk than indoor play, and this is sometimes given as a reason to restrict the times, activities and weather conditions for play out of doors. It would be wise to remember that in Scandinavia, young children spend large parts of the day out of doors, even in the winter, as they are warmly clothed and have appropriate footwear. Perhaps we should follow their example as we now know how important outdoor play is to children's development and their sense of wellbeing.

The QCA Guidance for the Foundation Stage states that

> Where possible, practitioners should allow children to move spontaneously between indoor and outdoor environments. Children will improve their co-ordination, control and ability to move more effectively if they can run, climb, balance, swing, slide, tumble, throw, catch and kick when they want to and are motivated and interested in doing so.
> *QCA, Curriculum Guidance for the Early Years Foundation Stage; QCA; 2000*

## Links with key Early Learning Goals:

Early Learning Goals which are linked to outdoor play are:

*Personal, social and emotional development*
- continue to be interested, excited and motivated to learn
- respond to significant experiences, showing a range of feelings when appropriate
- work as part of a group or class, taking turns and sharing fairly, understanding that there need to be agreed values, and codes of behaviour for groups of people, including adults and children, to work together harmoniously
- select and use activities and resources independently

*Communication, language and literacy*
- use language to imagine and recreate roles and experiences
- interact with others, negotiating plans and activities and taking turns in conversations
- attempt writing for various purposes, using features of different forms such as lists,
- stories, instructions
- write their own names and labels and form sentences, sometimes using punctuation

*Problem solving, reasoning and numeracy*
- use everyday words to describe position

*Knowledge and understanding of the world*
- find out about and identify some features of living things, objects and events they observe
- ask questions about why things happen and how things work
- build and construct with a wide range of objects, selecting appropriate resources, and adapting their work where necessary
- observe, find out and identify features in the place they live and the natural world

*Physical development*
- move with confidence, imagination and in safety
- move with control and co-ordination
- show awareness of space, of themselves and others
- use a range of small and large equipment
- travel around, under, over and through balancing and climbing equipment.

There are very few activities and resources which cannot be used outside, and most activities are enhanced by the outdoors. The opportunities to set up, share and reorganise activities are endless. If children are encouraged to get out their own apparatus and equipment from trolleys, sheds, baskets and boxes, they will always use it more imaginatively than if we decide for them. As well as the more familiar wheeled and climbing toys, open-ended resources such as ropes, posts, screens, plastic boxes, sheets and signs should be offered as they all increase independent thinking and action. Children will improvise from given materials to make others. They will use static equipment to support and extend temporary structures, and they will incorporate wheeled toys into their play, improving daily on what they have done before.

Apart from the physical dimension, outdoor play gives endless opportunities for social play: learning how to negotiate, co-operate and share equipment and games and how to work in a group, to take turns, to

*Independent Learning in the Foundation Stage*

delay their own gratification in the interests of others. The outside is often the only place where children can make noise with their bodies and voices. Large apparatus and wheeled toys encourage physical development, necessary for the co-ordination of eye, ear, hand and foot. The use of small apparatus further refines motor skills – throwing, catching, bouncing, rolling – and the chance to run, jump, hop, roll, skip, push and pull give the opportunity to revel in space and the freedom to move.

Children will also want to bring the inside out and the outside in – if we give them ownership of their play. They can bring out activities and equipment sometimes reserved for indoors – mark making, writing, books and other table-top activities in trays, on rugs or on tables; number games, drawing, collage and story telling are all suitable. Paint, dough, sand, woodwork and other messy materials can be available where there is space for collaborative or large-scale works. Small world, farm, jungle and zoo animals and vehicles all have a place, where chalk or paint can provide instant roads, fields and enclosures. Quiet areas, sensory gardens, flowers, bird tables, weather watching, small ponds and wild areas encourage interest in and care of the natural environment.

## Getting started with independence in outdoor play

- Make sure your storage area is as accessible as possible.
- If your storage is difficult for children to access, photograph all your equipment and make a photo book so the children can choose in advance what they want to play with.
- Look at the balance of wheeled toys and other activities to make sure these do not dominate or restrict the play.
- Look at the balance of hard and soft surfaces, so play can continue when the weather is bad.
- Try to find some way of providing covered areas (even if these are small) so children can be outside even in wet weather.
- Use bags and small containers for storage so children can get the resources themselves.
- Look for furniture that can easily be taken outside – children's picnic sets can be folded or stacked for storage and will provide places for table top activities.
- Ask the children where they would like to put fixed items of apparatus. Change the layout together.
- Put up some simple storage outside – shelves and surfaces for writing and other standing activities.
- Provide some vertical surfaces for mark making or painting – blackboards, painting boards, fences and sheds all provide opportunities.

## Ideas for resources to support independence in outdoor play

- Screw white or blackboards to the wall or fence, making some of them big for collaborative work.
- Put up a batten of wood along a wall or fence, about a metre or so from the ground. Pin paper or card to the batten for painting, chalk or crayons.
- Offer a basket of playground chalk for games and pictures. Make or buy some clipboards and small chalk boards
- Buy cheap decorating brushes for water painting; plastic sprays for spray painting or rollers and scrapers for water or paint on flat surfaces.
- Offer ribbons, string and strips of fabric for tying in fences and bushes. Make flags, notices, signs and labels.
- Provide bags or small baskets so children can collect their own resources for outdoor play.
- Barrels, tyres, boxes, guttering and drainpipes, rope, planks and tubes cost little and encourage imagination.
- Lightweight fabrics and clips or clothes pegs make good shelters and screens.
- Look for end of summer bargains in pop up tents and gazebos for portable shelters for winter and summer.
- Provide small containers with different sets (dinosaurs, people, farm/zoo animals, cars, etc.) to use in different places (sand, water, table top, grass).
- Small versions of metal garden tools, brushes, pans, spades, etc. are much more rewarding than plastic.
- Use plants and climbing vegetables to screen off areas in your garden.
- Provide a digging area where children can just dig.
- In cooler weather, provide some sleeping bags to keep children's legs warm and dry as they sit outside. Try a PE or crash mat for boisterous tumbling play.
- Plan some surprises to promote language and exploration – for example a mirror, bubbles, streamers, footprints, a basket of new objects.
- Make bird boxes and feed the birds. Then provide somewhere quiet for bird watching.
- Use recycled railway sleepers or decking to make raised surfaces for sand play or play with small world figures.

*Independent Learning in the Foundation Stage*

## Managing storage and access

- Boxes and baskets, light enough for the children to carry.
- Small trolleys or vegetable baskets keep things like balls, bean bags, paints, toys, equipment for science & outdoor collage, garden tools, etc. safe.
- Fit hooks and shelves in your shed, so things can be hung up, and paint outlines of the objects so children can put them back in the right places.
- Child sized bags and baskets are good for clearing up (have several so they can all help).
- Have several smaller sheds, rather than one big one. Then you can store things in different ones to make access easier. You could use one for wheeled toys, with shelves above for prop boxes. Then, when the bikes are out, the shed can become a role play area.

## A case study of encouraging independence in outdoor play

When children feel comfortable in their outside area and are empowered to make decisions and select resources, they will be more confident and will get more engaged in the activities you offer. Consider the use of the outside environment in this account.

Brendon walks towards the outside door, which opens onto the patio area and the garden. As he passes Nazia, he says, 'Coming outside?' Nazia looks up from the train track, nods and joins him. The two children pause on the threshold to the garden to see what is going on outside. It's autumn, and although it's sunny the gusting wind sets the wind chimes ringing and swirls leaves across the garden. It feels cold.

'I'm getting my coat,' says Brendon. 'Do you want yours?' He fetches their coats and they put them on.

The play area is busy. Bikes are popular, and a group of children run with ribbons streaming from their hands. A basket of bean bags, small balls and quoits has been placed just outside the door. A small trolley with playground chalk, clipboards and mark makers is also at hand. A pop-up tent has been erected on the edge of the grass, with a prop basket of fabrics, assorted hats and bags and an old mobile phone.

Nazia runs back inside and soon reappears with some bubbles, which she and Brendon begin to blow. Other children come to join the game, jumping and racing to catch the bubbles. Ben (a nursery nurse) has been watching. He begins to talk about the colours in the bubbles and the way they are swept away by the wind. The children stand still and watch, commenting on what is happening.

After a while Brendon and Nazia give the bubbles to another child and go over to the edge of the hard playground, where leaves have been blown into a pile by the wind. They pick up handfuls of leaves and throw them into the air, watching as they

fly. Some sycamore seeds have also blown into the garden. Brendon knows about these. 'My dad calls these helicopters,' he says. 'Look how they fly.' He shows Nazia how to throw the seeds, and both children toss the seeds into the air, watching them spin and twirl. Brendon puts some seeds in his pocket to show the other children later.

Nazia says, 'I'm thirsty. I'm getting a drink. Are you coming?'

Brendon shakes his head. 'I'm going in the sand.'

Nazia fetches a drink from inside and brings it to the picnic table on the patio. She sits and watches the other children, content for a few minutes to just observe their play.

Meanwhile Brendon, Jake and Carly are building an animal park in the sand tray. They make cages for the animals with small sticks from the ground, and fetch some card from the trolley to make a notice for the park. Sonny approaches fast on his bike. He bangs into the sand tray and dislodges the notice. He rushes off again, leaving the three park constructors standing with their mouths open. Ben comes over and sympathises, helping them to repair and re-erect the notice before he goes off to have a word with Sonny.

A child rings a small bell to warn that it is time to pack up the toys. Everybody helps to collect the bikes, to return balls and quoits to the basket, to clean the blackboards which are fixed to the fence, and to untie the ribbons from the tree branches. Brendon takes the 'helicopter' seeds out of his pocket and sends one flying before going inside to join the group for a story.

These children were confident. They knew what they wanted to do, had ideas about how to do it, and knew they had the freedom to choose when, where and who to play with. They respected each other, listened to each other and worked together collaboratively – and when they didn't, a practitioner was on hand to defuse a potentially volatile situation and talk quietly to the child who had misbehaved. There was space for children to take time out to watch what was going on, and opportunities for them to experience natural materials such as leaves, twigs and seeds. At clearing-up time they worked as a team to put things away and prepare for the end of the session.

## Suggestions for giving your children ownership of outdoor play activities

- Don't put everything out for the children before they come out. Get them involved in what goes out and where it's put.
- When you buy resources, involve the children. Ask them what they need, let them help with choosing new equipment and apparatus.
- Boxes, planks, ropes, buckets and pulleys will give more scope for imagination than fixed apparatus. Watch for children's own ideas to emerge and, without intruding, encourage them to build on these.

*Independent Learning in the Foundation Stage*

- Let the children choose what to grow, and don't be afraid to let them experiment. You might not be able to grow bananas in Barking but you could let children plant seeds outdoors and indoors to see what happens! If you haven't got a garden, let them plant and care for seeds or bulbs in pots, window boxes and containers.
- Children love making their own dens and hidey-holes. Provide cardboard boxes or fabric sheets to attach to fixed apparatus or buildings.
- Encourage children to name and label their structures. Make sure there are plenty of opportunities to make their own signs, notices, flags, instructions, labels, badges, etc. to personalise their play.
- Involve the children in the location and timing of snacks and drinks, stories and circle time. Most children would rather be out of doors!
- Ask questions of the children to encourage them to use the resources and equipment imaginatively – for example, a small world set, some cars and some guttering have many possibilities.
- Be sensitive to new ideas to support and extend their play and respond to them when they arise.

## Questions to ask when you review the quality of outdoor play in your setting

- Is your outdoor area an exciting, flexible environment? Does it change frequently to meet the needs of the children and give them opportunities in many areas of learning?
- Are the children encouraged to change and adapt the outdoor areas, furniture, equipment, as they need for their play? Do you put everything out for the children, or could you involve them more in deciding what goes out and where?
- Do you consider versatility when choosing new equipment, making sure that new things have many possible uses, that they can be used by more than one child at a time and that children of different ages and stages can use them? Could you involve the children more in selecting and buying new equipment and apparatus?
- Is the outdoor storage accessible to the children? Can they help to get things out and put them away? Do you make full use of all the spaces available to you, such as sheds or other outdoor storage spaces when they are empty?
- Do you give opportunities for children to personalise their play by, for example, offering flexible resources with many uses and providing mark making equipment?

# Chapter 10:
# Construction

Construction using bricks, small construction sets and found materials is a feature in early years settings of all types and locations. Of course there are hundreds of different types of commercially produced construction resources, and most settings have a good range. Found materials are less frequently used, but these make useful additions and are particularly good for developing concentration and deep learning.

Using construction materials is one important way in which children practise and perfect fine motor control. Without good hand-eye co-ordination reading and writing are very difficult. However, the valuable contribution of construction activities to fine motor skill development is sometimes overlooked by busy practitioners, who are happier to have resources that are appealing to children without needing adult support. The construction area is sometimes a neglected area, considered by practitioners to be a place where 'children can get on by themselves'. Because of this, it is often where most independence is given to children in deciding how and what they do, and with whom. It is also the place where real learning and language development often take place, particularly for boys, and so should be a regular focus for observations by adults.

Recent research into brain development tells us that boys and girls develop different parts of their brains at different ages. From the beginning of nursery, boys will opt for practical activities, especially outdoors, and will choose frequent change. Girls of the same age will choose books, painting and drawing, and even at this stage they will spend twice as long on an activity as boys. This is because the left side of the brain (the side linked to analytical skills and language learning) develops earlier in girls than in boys. By providing a wide range of construction activities we help boys and girls to develop both sides of their brains. For girls, construction gives opportunities to work in three dimensions, in patterns and shapes with mathematical connections and in

> **Provide flexible resources that can be used in many different ways to facilitate children's play and exploration. These might include lengths of plastic guttering, tubing and watering cans near the sand and water play areas; lengths of fabric and clothes pegs in a box; large paintbrushes and buckets near the outside tap; boxes, clothes horses, old blankets and tablecloths to make dens and shelters.**
>
> *EYFS Practitioner Guidance (card 4.1);*
> *DCSF; May 2008*

right brain activities. It gives boys the chance to concentrate and to improve those essential skills, which come from the left brain.

Building with three-dimensional objects falls into three main areas:

- using bricks of various sizes and made from various materials.
- using joining sets like Lego, Sticklebricks, Mobilo.
- using recycled and found materials, such as cartons, card tubes, reels, spools, plastic containers and bottles, tops, string, wool, fabric, plastic, paper and card.

These materials can be used to make temporary or permanent structures.

## Links with key Early Learning Goals

*Personal, social and emotional development*
- maintain attention, concentration
- work as part of a group or class, taking turns and sharing fairly, understanding that there need to be agreed values and codes of behaviour for groups of people, including adults and children, to work together harmoniously

*Communication, language and literacy*
- use language to imagine and recreate roles and experiences

*Problem solving, reasoning and numeracy*
- use language such as more, less, greater, smaller, heavier, lighter to compare two numbers or quantities
- talk about, recognise and recreate simple patterns
- use language such as circle or bigger to describe the shape and size of solids and flat shapes
- use everyday words to describe position

*Knowledge and understanding of the world*
- investigate objects and materials by using all of their senses as appropriate
- build and construct with a wide range of objects, selecting appropriate resources, and adapting their work where necessary
- select tools and techniques they need to shape, assemble and join the materials they are using

*Physical development*
- move with confidence, imagination and in safety
- move with control and co-ordination use a range of small and large equipment
- handle tools, objects, construction and malleable materials safely and with increasing control

*Creative development*
- express and communicate their ideas, thoughts and feelings by using a widening range of materials, suitable tools, imaginative and role play, movement, designing and making, and a variety of songs and instruments

Many of the more permanent resources for construction need maintenance. Wooden blocks should be splinter free, stable to build with and well organised for access and storage. Regular varnishing will help to prolong their lives and protect the corners. Plastic and foam bricks should be cleaned regularly and stored in lightweight bags or crates so that children can carry them easily. Construction sets need regular washing, and should be refurbished by replacing damaged and missing parts and by adding new ones. Recycled materials must be well organised and labelled if they are not to become an uninspiring muddle, well described as 'junk'!

Each construction set needs a good mixture of standard parts and additions, such as wheels, roof tiles, arches, cogs and figures. Storing sets in several smaller containers is a way of enabling children to access them without help, and therefore enables them to be independent by working in smaller groups and different locations. Of course, children should be able to mix and combine different sets for more ambitious projects.

Construction with found materials needs thoughtful planning and organisation. It is important to make sure that glue and other joining materials, such as tape and staples, can be used independently. We need to encourage experiment without fear of failure, in an atmosphere where children go readily to each other and to adults for help, advice and guidance on the technological aspects of what they are making.

Space is vital for constructions of all sorts, and if possible there should be a place where work in progress can be left out overnight, or put aside while glue or paint are drying. Brick play needs a flat, soft surface inside or out. A large piece of carpet is ideal. Children often prefer to work with construction and found materials on tables or benches, and these areas can include a shelf for storing models and structures.

Time is all-important in planning construction activities. Children need that 'time for sustained concentration' (QCA), which gives them room to develop the play, process it in their minds and return to it later or even the next day. This is not always possible for every activity in every setting, but it is a principle that we should try to remember. Children haven't finished an activity just because we say it is time to pack away!

Construction activities contribute to all areas of learning. Their relevance can be seen in the collaborative aspects of personal development, in shape and space in maths, in science, technology, physical skills and creativity.

## Getting started with independence in construction play

- Talk about construction, encourage children to plan where they will start and what they might make.
- Is your construction area dominated by boys? If so, it's important to consider how what it offers can be made more interesting for girls. Often it doesn't take a great deal. Simply including small world people can be enough to stimulate girls' interest.
- Display books near construction areas to help children with ideas. These should include images of both sexes in construction and adventurous jobs. Put up posters or photos of buildings and vehicles near the construction area so children can be inspired to innovate in their building. Change these regularly.
- Make a photo or scrap book with examples of buildings and vehicles, children's plans and drawings of their own constructions, and photos of constructions, complete or unfinished, which have been made in your setting, both indoors and out.
- Some children love to mix different sorts of construction materials, or take them into other areas of the setting. This is a clear sign of independent learning, but you need to establish a clear understanding of the process!
- Adding cars and small world people will take the play in different directions. Make sure children know that it is acceptable to do this, by sometimes leaving them nearby.
- Add chalk or big sheets of paper and felt pens to the basket of bricks and cars.
- Put idea cards in the Lego box, and offer a camera to record what the children make, for a photo book.
- Use old, worn bricks, sticks, twigs, small logs or offcuts of wood to extend the recycled materials.
- Work with the children to use big bricks to make houses, shops, boats for full sized or small world role play.

## Ideas for resources to support independence in construction play

- Take Lego outside on a concrete mixing tray.
- Use a big sheet of card or wood as the base for a group construction with recycled materials.
- Try a construction that is on more than one level or surface – table to floor, down a step, under a table, on a plank supported above the ground.
- Sometimes have a week with no glue in the construction area.

- Use found materials to make temporary arrangements of objects, collages and buildings. Draw or photograph the results. Dismantle them afterwards.
- Offer cut card circles and split pins for wheels.
- Try to collect found materials that have their own colour, and remember that boxes and containers with printed words and pictures distract children from the form of the object.
- Avoid paint unless you can be sure that it will stick to the surfaces available!
- Masking tape is easier to use than sticky tape.
- Make sure the scissors are sharp enough to cut the materials available.
- In the technology area, offer small scale materials to make signs and notices – cocktail sticks, straws, plasticene, card, fine markers, photocopies of road and shop signs, pictures of people.
- Sets of people enhance play in any construction materials. Don't restrict the doll's house family to their own house! Construction can be the basis for story telling or re-telling.
- Make constructions such as beds, dens and shelters for soft toys and dolls.
- Challenge children to make a construction that uses a limited number of pieces, or a limited range of shapes or colours.
- Add some more unusual items or fasteners such as paper plates, clothes pegs, straws, computer labels, Christmas tape, cellophane, shredded paper, packing materials, bubble wrap etc.
- Offer natural materials such as garden sticks, twigs, plant pots, hay, leaves and seeds.
- Construct dens and shelters outside, and add extensions to fixed climbing apparatus, using boxes, tubes etc.
- Use string, rope and fabric to make full size and miniature tents for children or toys.

## Managing storage and access

- All construction materials need to be both plentiful and manageable. It's better to have several small boxes or baskets that children can carry, rather than a huge box that can't be moved.
- Lightweight boxes or baskets are cheap and easy for children to carry.
- Construction materials are best stored near the places where children choose to play – observe where they take the construction and consider whether you need to alter the layout of your room.
- Use 'builders' trays' on floors or in outside areas, so smaller pieces don't get lost.

*Independent Learning in the Foundation Stage*

# A case study of encouraging independence in construction

Here is an example of good use of construction materials. The children have plenty of opportunities to control and shape the activities, and these naturally flow into a range of experiences which the teacher had not planned. Note how she acts as a resource, providing just the right amount of stimulation and encouragement to keep things moving forward.

The room is set up with clearly defined areas for different activities. Four children (three boys and a girl) are playing on a carpeted area with a large set of small wooden bricks. They have made a huge layout of the bricks in a complicated design of roads, buildings, trees, parks and fields. As they work, individuals fetch additional resources – a basket of farm animals, a village set, some cars and play people. Other children come to watch the construction as it grows, and some ask if they can join in. They are made welcome and they contribute more ideas as they get involved in the play. The practitioner observes as the construction develops. She says nothing, but makes notes and takes a series of photos as the construction grows over the day.

At clearing up time at the end of the day, the children ask if they can leave their village until the next day, as they have some more ideas for additions. The group discuss this, as the village is right in the middle of the carpet area used for group time. The other children are very accommodating and make suggestions for managing, such as 'We could squash up, so we don't knock anything over' or 'We could have stories and singing outside instead'. So the village continues to expand over several days with different children involved. At group times the adults encourage the children to talk about the construction, modelling language and vocabulary, suggesting books and stories that might be of interest.

One day one practitioner offers a set of road signs. This sparks new enthusiasm, and a flurry of writing follows. Children use materials in the technology area to make signs and notices, including one to the premises officer saying 'plese kep off'. The children select small sticks, plastic bottle tops and pieces of card from the carefully organised boxes of materials, each clearly labelled with its contents, to make more signs. They give the village a name: 'Brickland'.

Martha fetches a peaked cap and a shoulder bag from the prop box. She has been to a safari park and knows about tickets. She makes some from paper, cutting them out very carefully. She uses crayons to decorate each one and stands by a box of play money and a notice which says 'brikland pay here'. The play develops into another phase.

Eventually the work on the village expands into all areas of the curriculum, providing opportunities in maths, language, science, technology, for visits and walks in the locality and for the development of fine motor skills. The extended building and reorganisation of the construction involves plenty of opportunity for developing social skills such as negotiation and compromise.

These children were relaxed and comfortable with an independent activity, negotiating with other children and adults, and collecting resources for play from all over the setting. They enjoy the concentrated play that comes form continuing an activity over several days, and are happy when

the impetus for the play runs out and the group is ready to move on to something else. The adults are also relaxed about longer projects and play scenarios, using observation to support and expand the play, and involving the whole group in decisions.

## Suggestions for giving your children ownership of construction activities

- The case study described an on-going activity in construction. Try to make room for a place where children can leave their unfinished work and precious constructions in Lego or other materials.
- Encourage children to mix and combine construction materials. Offer small baskets or bags for collecting resources, and teach them to return these when they have finished playing.
- Take time and care when organising found and recycled materials for children. Transparent containers and helpful labels make access easier.
- Encourage flexibility in working. Blur the edges between areas and activities, so children can move easily from construction to mark making, from inside to outside.
- Observe and document their play, and feed back what you see by sharing photos and writing down their words.
- Record their constructions through photos and drawings. The records can then be displayed with books and posters and children's own words.
- Help those who are less confident to get involved by encouraging them to make labelled diagrams, signs and notices.

## Questions to ask when you review the quality of construction play in your setting

- Do you give this area of the curriculum the status it deserves? Do you visit it, observe it and include it in your discussions and group times where children report back on their activities?
- Are the resources for construction well-organised, attractive, well maintained, high quality? Are there enough of them?
- Are children encouraged to develop the play? Are you able to leave unfinished or ongoing constructions overnight or over longer periods?
- Do children feel comfortable combining sets of equipment to extend their play? Can children move from area to area, following their needs to make marks, integrate other materials, revisit activities, refer to books?
- Do children have the tools, materials and support to help them be successful when working on bigger or more permanent constructions? Does the glue really stick? Are the scissors sharp enough?

# Chapter 11:
# Storytelling

Stories play a crucial role in the development of young children, and we now know that children who hear, tell and play plenty of stories in their early years will usually become enthusiastic readers. When children listen to a story they engage in an active process that impacts on their thinking and influences their perceptions of themselves and the world in which they live. Practitioners need to ensure that, through the stories they offer, children have the opportunity to experience a range of approaches, attitudes and responses to life. As children engage with the characters in the story they explore the experiences of others, and as part of this process relate what is happening to others to the things they have experienced in their own lives.

Stories have many functions and effects. They communicate messages, make statements about right and wrong, suggest ways of going about things and set up expectations. In short, stories have the potential to profoundly influence the way children behave.

When we choose stories and texts for young children we must think carefully about the messages that we are transmitting. If children are exposed to a diet of stories where the heroes and heroines sit about waiting for someone else to take responsibility for sorting out their problems, then we must expect this to influence the way they respond to problems and difficulties themselves. If, on the other hand, the stories they hear feature strong, empowered characters ready and willing to take responsibility for the things that happen in their lives, then we are probably looking at very different outcomes.

Let's take the familiar story of Cinderella. Cinderella is a victim, picked on by her ugly sisters and exploited by her family. In fact, without the support of the fairy godmother she would probably have been condemned to live out her days in a dingy basement as a servant to her family. As she waits for her prince, she is powerless. Her destiny is in the hands of her family, and she does not expect that life will ever be any different. When her circumstances suddenly change, and she is whisked away by a handsome prince, no-one is more surprised than she. But if we were to write the sequel to this story, what might happen to poor Cinderella? If in the future she is faced with difficult circumstances, how will she cope? Suppose the prince fell on hard times and took up with a rich widow as a means of solving his

problems; what would become of Cinderella then? It seems more than likely that she would have to return to the kitchen!

Cinderella is just one example of the messages conveyed by traditional stories. Think about some of the others – Aladdin, Jack and the Beanstalk, Sleeping Beauty – and try a similar analysis of your own. We are not condemning traditional stories or saying that they should not be used. On the contrary, they are great fun and part of children's heritage. But it is important to be aware not only of the simple narrative line but also of what the stories are saying beneath the surface, and to ensure that children are also exposed to other material which offers alternative views.

In recent years there have been many alternative versions of traditional tales that challenge the archetypal view of the heroine as passive victim or the hero as handsome playboy. Some titles you may like to try are: *Little Red Riding Hood: A Newfangled Prairie Tale* by Lisa Campbell Ernst or *Mixed Up Fairy Tales* by Hilary Robinson and Nick Sharratt.

> All this is crucial for how young children develop their powers of thinking and understanding. At the same time, it's how they get to feel good about themselves. The two things are intertwined – feeling good about yourself, feeling confident enough to develop your thinking and understanding.
>
> *Michael Rosen (Children's Laureate) in Every Child a Talker; DCSF; 2008*

## Links with key Early Learning Goals

*Communication, language and literacy:*

- enjoy listening to and using spoken and written language, and readily turn to it in their play and learning
- explore and experiment with sounds, words and texts
- listen with enjoyment and respond to stories, songs and other music, rhymes and poems and make up their own stories, songs, rhymes
- use language to imagine and recreate roles and experiences
- use talk to organise, sequence and clarify thinking, ideas, feelings and events
- sustain attentive listening, responding to what they have heard by relevant comments, questions or actions
- extend their vocabulary, exploring the meanings and sounds of new words
- retell narratives in the correct sequence, drawing on the language patterns of stories

Wherever we go we can see storytelling in action: in shops, cafés, bars, on buses and on street corners people are telling their stories. Storytelling is an integral part of life and human relationships. Our stories are our identity, and as we tell them we make sense of things that have happened to us, refine our judgements, modify our point of view and reflect upon our values. In short, our stories assist us in learning more about who we are. It is through our stories that we learn about ourselves, and the world in which we live. This is just as important for children as it is for adults. Stories have great potential for enhancing children's self-knowledge and self-esteem.

The stories that mean most to us as adults are those which relate to our personal experience and view of the world. Others, of course, provide escape from or a contrast with our own lives, or inhabit a world of make believe and fantasy, but children do not acquire these more sophisticated tastes until later. It is important to make sure that the subject matter of the stories we tell is designed to really engage the children, so we need to be aware of the issues that matter to young children and present these with flair and sensitivity. The use of soft toys and puppets can really help us to do just that. The puppet is a very potent tool, as it can stimulate the imagination, extend vocabulary and help young children to move from telling stories based on their own experiences into the realm of the imagination. Puppets are tangible; children can experience them through their senses. They can see them and touch them, identify with them, and have no difficulty suspending their disbelief.

Large humanoid puppets are now readily available in most of the catalogues of the major education suppliers, and they are not difficult to use. You do not need to be theatrical or extrovert. Simply sit the puppet on a chair and let the story making begin. The moment you introduce children to a puppet you will find that they engage with it on an emotional level, and when the emotions are engaged the learning is always deeper. Some practitioners feel embarrassed when manipulating a doll or puppet. Don't be. The children will be watching and talking to the doll, not you!

Children can be involved at all stages of the process, making decisions about what the doll or puppet should be called, where they live, who they live with and the things they like to do. In a very short space of time they will become cult figures in your setting and their personalities will continue to evolve as more and more stories develop. The events in which they figure and the things that happen to them can mirror things that are important to the children, helping them with their own storying.

If you introduce some familiar moral dilemmas you can provide even more encouragement for independence. For example, disobeying the

instructions of a parent or teacher (either consciously or unconsciously), going somewhere they have been told not to go, or taking something that does not belong to them.

This work is both rewarding and interesting, and an excellent way of using imaginative material to develop children's independent thinking. Open-ended stories present scenarios which have no simple right or wrong answer. They enable you to review all the possibilities and go with what your reasoning tells you is right. These are skills vital to the development of independence.

## Getting started with independence in story making and storytelling

- Read or tell stories in which children act independently, take responsibility, show initiative and solve problems.
- Make time for children to tell you their stories and be excited about what they have to say.
- Share your own stories with the children. Tell them about things that have happened to you.
- Record children's stories on tape, and in writing. This gives them real value and offers lots of opportunities for talking.
- Encourage children to share their own experiences and stories. Ask questions which will encourage them to talk about times when they have used their initiative to solve a problem or accomplished something through their own efforts.
- Make the children's stories into books and put them in the book corner or class library.
- Use puppets to model stories about characters showing independence and autonomy.
- Use puppets or soft toys to re-tell the events of the day or to explore difficulties or disputes.
- Take photos and make photo sequences of children's own stories or the adventures of puppets or soft toys.
- Re-tell favourite stories as children act them out. Help them to make simple props or costumes but don't make it a performance!

## Ideas for resources to support independence in storytelling

- Make up story boxes containing interesting things to stimulate storytelling – dinosaurs, space, under the sea, in the jungle, at the zoo, the seaside, etc.
- Decorate the insides of boxes for themes such as pirates or jungles.

- Make collections of artefacts. Try old maps, keys, binoculars, coins, etc.
- Set up a listening corner where children can select and listen to story tapes. Have a tape recorder so children can record their own stories.
- Collect a wide range of puppets which children can use for storybuilding.
- If you have an interactive whiteboard, use this for storytelling, using clip art or imported photos or drawings.
- Cut out some pictures from old books or magazines and mount them on card. Play a game by picking out three and making up a story around them. Do it yourself a few times to show the children how, and they'll soon pick up the idea.
- Before the children arrive for the session, put an object or artefact in the middle of the room e.g. a very large cardboard box, some sparkly material, a pile of conkers. Ask them who they think could have left them. Encourage them to use their imaginations and suggest unusual ideas.
- Sit in a quiet place in your setting and be a resource yourself, telling or recording children's stories.
- Make a place in your garden or outdoor area where children can play out stories.
- Provide some pictures from catalogues, worn out books, magazines etc and let the children use these to make their own story books.
- Offer simple story bags for children to take home to share with parents. Just a book and a simple resource or toy will make the story much easier to tell.
- Make sure story books are evident in all areas of your setting, to inspire links with other activities and areas of learning.
- Expand your book collection by using local libraries and book collections.

## A case study of encouraging independence and involvement in storytelling

Consider the power of story in this account of an accident in a play setting and how, given support and encouragement, a child can turn any event into a story. The way adults react to children's own stories is vital if they are to gain confidence and self-knowledge for everyday experiences.

Lee was having a really good time in the soft play area. With a group of friends he had built an elaborate obstacle course and was enjoying himself crawling, leaping and balancing on and through a range of self-constructed challenges. The children's pleasure was obvious as they urged each other on and shrieked with the pure enjoyment of it all. Suddenly the shrieks of delight were pierced by a scream. Lee had fallen from a piece of equipment and was howling loudly as he grasped one hand in the other. As he had fallen, Lee had landed on his hand and bent his finger

back. The teacher sent for the first-aider, who advised that Lee should be taken to hospital to have his injured finger checked out.

All the arrangements were made. Lee was to go to the hospital accompanied by a teacher, and his mother would meet them there. Although Lee had initially been somewhat distraught he eventually calmed down and warmed to the idea of a trip out of school. Once on his way he was full of curiosity about everything around him. At the hospital he engaged first the receptionist, then the nurse and finally the doctor in a full and frank account of everything that had happened to him.

The doctor explained that Lee would have to have an X-ray to find out whether his finger was broken. Would he be able to see the pictures? Lee wanted to know. On his way to be X-rayed he showed yet more curiosity, asking questions throughout and commenting on every stage of the process.

By the time his mother arrived, looking ashen faced and worried, she must have wondered what all the fuss was about. A beaming Lee greeted her with an enthusiastic invitation to view the pictures of his finger 'to see if it was broked!'

When the X-ray was finally displayed Lee was fascinated. He could hardly believe that what he was looking at was what was 'inside his hand'. Fortunately nothing was broken, and all that was required was a sturdy bandage, which Lee wore with pride and pleasure.

By this time, his mum was keen to take him home but Lee was having none of it, insisting that he return to school. Once there, what ensued was to stun everyone. Lee held the attention of ten adults and a hundred children as he told the story of everything that had happened from beginning to end in copious detail. As he did so he grew visibly, gaining confidence as well as pleasure from telling his own story.

This account is something we can all relate to. Every practitioner has stories of accidental injury in their setting. Despite all the care we take, independent children will take risks as they play and sometimes accidents happen. How we respond, and how resilient the child is can turn a frightening experience into an adventure, worth telling to others.

## Suggestions for giving your children ownership of storytelling

- Send a letter to the children from a fictional character or a soft toy, creating a situation to which they can make a response. For example: Spot could be on his holidays and want the children to help him record his adventures when he returns; Kipper might like to have a birthday party; The Three Bears may be fed up with porridge and want advice about other things to have for breakfast.
- Wrap up a parcel and have it delivered to the classroom by the site supervisor or secretary. The children can try to guess the contents and, once they have opened the parcel, who it has come from and why it has come to them.

*Independent Learning in the Foundation Stage*

- Make a collection of old photos and pictures of interesting characters. Encourage children to make up stories around them.
- Plan a storytelling event, or invite storytellers into your setting.
- Read the work of Vivian Gussin Paley, a practitioner who makes children's own stories to life through retelling and acting them out or refer to *Stories for Young Children* (Featherstone).
- Start telling a story yourself and get the children to carry it on and finish it off. You could start with a story they know and move on to stories you and they make up.
- Make books in which the children are the main characters and allow them to make decisions about content, text and format.
- Tell group stories, encouraging the children to contribute ideas drawn from things they have done and events they have experienced; e.g. the day our class/group went to the zoo, forest, seaside, etc.
- Use a small mat or rug as a magic carpet. Let one of the children sit on it and encourage the others to contribute ideas about where it is going and how it will get there, describing the journey as it progresses.
- Get the children to make a display of their favourite stories. Encourage them to talk about the ones they have chosen and what they particularly like about them.

## Questions to ask when you review the quality of storytelling opportunities in your setting

- Are children involved in decisions about which stories will be read and told? Are they encouraged to develop a critical response to the stories they hear? Are they consulted about which new storybooks should be purchased?
- Do adults model the storytelling process? How often do you as practitioners 'act out' stories for the children?
- Are children's stories really valued by adults? How do you show this? Do you accept children's storytelling contributions without judgement, allowing them to develop their expertise over time?
- Do you help parents and carers to understand the value of story to children's development?
- What are you doing to improve your own storytelling skills?

# Chapter 12:
# Writing

The Guidance for the EYFS suggests that we should be giving children opportunities to see adults speaking, listening, reading and writing. In an earlier chapter we emphasised the importance of example, and it is worth repeating it again here. Children pick up their attitudes to learning from what they observe of adults, so it is clear that we should be demonstrating for them in our daily behaviour the communication skills we want them to acquire. We should immerse them 'in an environment rich in print and possibilities for communication', encouraging them 'to recognise the importance of written language through signs, notices and books.' (QCA)

The EYFS Guidance also advises that children should have chances to share and enjoy a wide range of stories, poems, rhymes and non fiction books, to experiment with writing through mark making and to begin to understand how print works.

Mark making and writing activities are some of the best ways of promoting independence and autonomy. Even in this age of ICT, writing by hand is still an important activity. Children who have good access to high quality equipment, choice, freedom, support and recognition for their efforts will become writers. Just as children need free access to play materials and the outside environment, they need access to materials and equipment for mark making, an environment rich in print, and a place where they have models of adults and other children as writers. Learning about the purposes of writing is part of the process of becoming a writer, and the best way to learn about the purposes of writing is to write, to see others writing and to practise mark making and writing activities in real-life situations at home, within the setting, in the local community and in role-play of all sorts.

Children learn by doing. They learn to talk by talking, they learn to read by reading and they learn to write by writing. Of course, they eventually need to learn the orthodox way of forming letters and they need to realise that

> Within the context of an active play-based learning environment, children will have many different ways of representing their thoughts and feelings in the early years. Some will choose music, dance or song, others will prefer to tell stories through role-play, drama or using small world resources, but most will at some point be naturally drawn to represent their ideas graphically. When children realise that marks can be used symbolically to carry meaning, in much the same way as the spoken word, they begin to use marks as tools to make their thinking visible.
>
> *Mark Making Matters; DCSF; 2008*

*Independent Learning in the Foundation Stage*

writing has meaning which can be interpreted by the reader, but in the beginning stages of writing children need the freedom to experiment with this activity in the same way as they do with every other. They need to explore, try out, practise, adapt and expand. They need to compare the marks they make with the writing they see. As in all their learning, at first the process is much more important than the product.

## Links with key Early Learning Goals

Goals associated with writing are found throughout the six areas as well as in Communication, Language and Literacy. Here are some of the key ones:

*Communication, language, and literacy*
- enjoy listening to and using spoken and written language, and readily turn to it in their play and learning
- explore and experiment with sounds, words and texts
- attempt writing for various purposes, using features of different forms such as lists, stories, instructions
- write their own names and labels and form sentences, sometimes using punctuation
- use their phonic knowledge to write simple regular words and make phonetically plausible attempts at more complex words
- use a pencil effectively and hold it effectively to form recognisable letters, most of which are correctly formed

*Physical development*
- handle tools, with increasing control

*Creative development*
- express and communicate their ideas, thoughts and feelings by using a widening range of materials.

If the materials, models and equipment are regularly available to them, children's first experiences of writing will usually be in role-play or at writing tables, writing messages, labels, lists and letters. If every role-play situation, inside and outside, offers materials for writing and mark making they will be used. If every adult in the setting models writing as a useful and important activity, if they talk about what they are writing, if they read back observations, explain messages and letters, make lists with the children, write recipes, transcribe the children's thoughts and descriptions of work to use as captions and labels, then children will begin to make the link between what is spoken and what is written.

If every visitor and every visit involves children in writing lists, notes and letters; if children's attention is drawn to writing in offices, shops, surgeries, fire stations, garages, the school or setting; if children have the

opportunity and resources to replicate the sort of writing they see being done by their parents and by practitioners (e.g. by offering forms, notebooks and diaries) they will use these experiences in their own play. The aim is for children to begin to see the relationship between their own writing and the writing they see around them.

Writing materials and equipment should echo the quality resource indicators discussed in Chapter 4. Here is a simple checklist which practitioners may find useful:

**Access** – Are the writing materials easy to access?

**Organisation** – Are they clearly grouped and labelled so children can find them and put them away?

**Presentation** – Are things carefully and attractively stored, so children can see what is on offer?

**Condition** – Are things checked for missing pieces, cleanliness, broken boxes, etc.? Are they topped up so there is always plenty of choice?

**Manageability** – Are writing implements appropriate to the ages and stages of development of the children? For example, are there different sizes of pencils, pens, crayons and scissors?

**Location** – Are things located near the play base where they are likely to be used?

**Quality** – Is the writing and mark making equipment of the highest possible quality that the setting can afford? Are we insistent on the best for the children?

**Suitability** – Are the resources suitable for the purpose and the children? Do the scissors actually cut, are pencils sharp?

**Sufficiency** – Is there enough of everything – scissors, staplers, envelopes?

**Range** – Do we have a good range of equipment for boys and girls, to reflect diversity and the local community, to meet special needs?

## Getting started with independence in writing

- 'Plant' a letter from a story book or local character in the room for the children to find; link writing ideas with story books.
- Write invitations and thank you letters to visitors; encourage everyone you know to send you and the children postcards and letters.
- Scribe children's comments to put with their pictures and models; each time you put up a new caption, sign or notice, read it with the children.
- Make lists of things to do, or what you need for a project or visit.
- Explain the writing *you* do (registers, notes, messages and reminders, labels) to the children; bring your personal writing to share – letters, cards, lists, instructions, diaries.
- With the children, collect examples of different sorts of writing – lists, forms, labels, instructions as well as stories, poems, diaries, letters.

- Make suggestions for writing recipes, menus, poems, recording weather, attendance, celebrating birthdays and other special events; put forms and junk mail in home corners.
- Suggest that children write reminders and messages for themselves.
- Some ideas for writing:
  - A café or coffee shop with bills, menus and pads for the waiters and waitresses.
  - A bus with home-made bus tickets.
  - A doctor's surgery with prescriptions.
  - A fire station with a message pad.
  - A hairdressers with appointment cards and appointment book.
  - An office with a computer, letters and envelopes.
  - A takeaway pizza place with message pads, orders and delivery notes.

## Ideas for resources to support independence in mark making and writing

Try to make available:
- Paper and card in a range of colours
- Several sizes of envelopes (recycled ones are fine)
- A range of sizes, types and colours of pens, pencils, crayons
- A letter writing table with a post box for children to send letters to each other and to the adults in the setting
- Sticky labels, badges
- Address books, diaries, calendars, appointment books
- Ready-made books (2 or 3 sheets stapled together) for stories
- Old keyboards, computers with word processing facilities
- Stamps - you can make your own by running a sewing machine (no cotton!) across paper to make perforations - then draw the pictures
... and some ideas for outside
- Clip boards for scoring games.
- Playground chalk for marking directions and messages.
- Signs, labels, notices and instructions.
- Spotter sheets for nature watching
- Small chalk boards or white boards
- A big blackboard screwed to the wall

## Managing storage and access

- Use vegetable baskets or small storage racks for different sorts of resources.
- Make some 'writing belts' like tool belts, or writing aprons with pockets, for outdoor writing.
- Put a basket of writing materials just inside or outside the door to the garden.
- Small plastic buckets make good storage pots for mark making resources.

## A case study of encouraging independence in writing and mark making

This case study shows how, when they have the resources and inspiration, children will naturally make their own 'meaningful marks'. David, Paddy and Shahida clearly know some of the purposes of writing, and use them in their play and learning in the well resourced and independent learning environment that is their setting.

David and Shahida are in the domestic role-play area. David is dressed as the mum, Shahida is dressed as a nurse. She is visiting the house to see the new baby. In her nurse's bag she has a notebook, a pen and a mobile phone.

Shahida examines the baby. She looks carefully in the baby's ears, listens to his chest and gives him an 'injection'. David asks, 'Is he OK?' 'Yes,' says Shahida. 'I'll give you a letter so you can show your husband.' She gets out her notebook and writes a note. Then she folds it up and gives it to David, who offers her a cup of tea. As he puts the note in his pocket he says, 'Your phone is ringing.'

Shahida answers the phone. 'Just a minute,' she says. 'I need to write the address down.' She writes some numbers and letters on her pad. 'I can't have a cup of tea, I've got to go to the hospital.'

Shahida leaves the house. She crosses the room and stops at the writing table, leaning over to watch her friend Paddy, who is making a card for his grandma's birthday. He has chosen a piece of orange card from the range on offer, some sequins and some feathers. He uses these to make the front of the card, saying as he works, 'This is a flower for my Nan. This is the leaves, and this is the sun – there, it's finished.' He notices Shahida watching him. 'Do you wanna make one? It's for my Nan. I'm gonna write inside when its dry.' Shahida shakes her head. She continues on her way across the room, meeting one of the adults and two children in aprons as she goes. 'Do you want to come and make some biscuits with us?' they say.

Shahida can't resist this invitation to join the cooking group, saying she'll go to the hospital later. She helps to read the pictorial recipe and to follow the steps it contains. When she has finished, she returns to the writing table, draws a picture of the cooking session and writes the names of the children in the group over each head, using her emerging knowledge of phonics to identify the first letter of each name. Underneath the picture she writes her own name and the word 'Bscts'. She takes her picture to one of the adults, who reads it with her and helps her to pin it on the low-level display board by the writing table.

Meanwhile, Paddy has returned to the writing corner to check on his card. It is dry, so he carefully opens it and inside he writes

'GrnHappyBrfdy
Lovefrom Paddy
XXXXXX'

He finds an envelope in the envelope drawer and writes 'Grn' on the outside. He puts the card into the envelope and takes it to his coat peg, where he balances it on top of his coat, 'So I don't forget to take it.'

The many opportunities to write and make marks, the easily available resources and the models provided by the practitioners in this setting all contribute to the way the children behave. David, Paddy and Shahida all get involved in writing in a very natural 'real-life' way, and the adults who work with them observe their learning carefully and respond by adding or adapting resources to extend their interests.

## Suggestions for giving your children ownership of their mark making

- Make the writing corner or table part of every day. Involve the children in the contents, organisation and location. Model writing by joining the children in this area, doing and talking about your own writing.
- Make sure the resources in the writing corner are interesting and easy to access. Change or add to the resources from time to time to sustain interest and give new ideas.
- Offer to act as scribe for their stories, captions, thoughts and comments.
- Value their writing. Put up a pin board at child height and encourage them to pin up their own writing. Encourage them to talk about their displays.
- With the children, collect examples of different sorts of writing. Look at lists, forms, labels, instructions as well as stories, poems, diaries, letters – so they experience a wide range of purposes for writing. Help them to make their own collections.
- Invite a local writer to come and talk about their work.
- Make sure there are invitations to mark make in your role play area, construction, book corner and outdoor area.

## Questions to ask when you review the quality of mark making and writing in your setting

- Do you have a writing/mark making area as a standard feature in your setting? Does the equipment in your writing area meet the quality criteria above? Do you offer a wide range of materials?
- Are the children encouraged to write as part of their play? Do you include writing in every role-play situation?
- Do you provide models of adults as writers? What could you do to improve the models you give? Do you explain and share the writing you do as adults?
- Do you exploit possibilities in stories, visits, visitors and the community to explore the purposes for writing?
- Do you promote 'emergent' writing and writers? Do you value process or product in writing? What is the balance in your setting between child-initiated and adult-directed writing?

# Chapter 13:
# Music, movement and dance

To watch young children as they respond to and explore music, sound and movement is a magical experience. They will frequently sing and dance quite spontaneously and with few inhibitions. Running, jumping, singing, shouting, swinging and swirling come easily and naturally. The role of early years practitioners is to keep that spontaneity alive and provide experiences and materials that enable children to build on these early explorations.

Perhaps for some of us, when we were young our earliest attempts to explore movement and sound were laughed at, leaving our confidence and self-esteem bruised, and resulting in inhibition in the face of music and dance. When this happens to children they grow up unable to sing anywhere else but the bathroom and willing to dance only in private! If we are to avoid this happening we must approach music, movement and dance with great sensitivity. While only a small minority of children will go on to become professional dancers and musicians, all children can dance and make music, and the experiences they encounter in early years settings should help to ensure that they continue to do so for the rest of their lives.

Working with movement and sound enables children to develop skills, concepts and attitudes across a range of contexts. It offers opportunities to develop creativity and imagination; language, social, observation, listening, attention, memory, counting and mathematical skills; concentration ... and much, much more. These activities offer rich opportunities, and when the children are able to take on some of the responsibility for organising their own experiences then the learning is truly enhanced.

The best practice will exist within a culture of shared control and will show a sensitive balance between adult-initiated and child-initiated activities. Once we have provided the appropriate materials our role as adults is that of 'kick starting' the children by introducing them to activities that enable them to see the potential of the resources. We then need to take a back seat and allow them to explore in their own way. At this point they need our sensitive support. By observing the ways in which they work with

> **Give opportunities for children to work alongside artists and other creative adults so that they see at first hand different ways of expressing and communicating ideas and different responses to media and materials.**
>
> *EYFS Principles into Practice cards 'Creative Development'; DCSF; 2008*

the materials we will be able to judge what other opportunities should be made available to them, and work out strategies for moving them on with their explorations.

## Links with key Early Learning Goals

The Early Learning Goals which are particularly relevant to music, movement and dance are:

*Personal, social & emotional development*
- continue to be interested, excited & motivated to learn

*Physical development*
- move with confidence, imagination and in safety
- move with control and co-ordination
- show awareness of space, themselves and others

*Creative development*
- Express and communicate their ideas, thoughts and feelings by using a widening range of materials, suitable tools, imaginative role-play, movement, designing and making, and a variety of songs and musical instruments.
- Explore colour, texture, shape, form and space in two and three dimensions
- Recognise and explore how sounds can be changed, sing simple songs from memory, recognise repeated sounds and sound patterns, and match movements to music
- Respond in a variety of ways to what they see, hear, smell, touch, and feel
- Use their imagination in art and design, music, dance, imagination and role play, and stories

For young children, movement and sound are very closely linked. When they hear music they often begin, quite spontaneously, to move to the sound and rhythm. When they are moving and dancing they will frequently make sounds to accompany their movement. Children in the early years are developing their musical awareness and skills with great speed. They have increasing control over their voices, can play simple rhythm instruments and are beginning to understand concepts of tempo, beat, melody and pitch. They are also starting to enjoy making music as part of a group.

Most children are fascinated by anything that makes a noise. Look in any shop which sells toys for the very young, almost everything there will make a sound of some sort. Manufacturers do not do this for nothing. Watch the way young children examine and investigate new objects. As well as tasting and feeling, they bang and shake to see if any sound results, and

when they do find things that can produce a musical note or two, observe their delight.

Introduce the children to new instruments. You don't have to be an expert in playing them – just able to raise a sound. Try to introduce the children to musicians, both professional and amateur. Make collections of tapes and CDs so that children can listen to a wide range of music from a variety of cultures. Share control with the children, allowing them to take the lead, as and when they feel ready.

Basic timing and a mastery of steady beat appears to be necessary to any task that involves sophisticated movement, and where a person lacks beat awareness he or she usually demonstrates a motor skill deficiency. In fact, recent studies show a correlation between beat competency and school achievement that exceeds two other major predictors of academic success – social class and mother's education. Practitioners have little control over the latter, but there is much we can do to support children's mastery of steady beat. By modelling and sharing action songs and rhymes and working with musical instruments we can make a real difference.

Many researchers and early years workers are currently interested in the links between early movement experiences and future learning. If we accept this astonishing link, that sensory stimulation of the sort provided by movement and dancing has an actual physical effect on the structure of the brain, there are important implications for our settings. We need to look at the opportunities that we provide for movement play, and at how we support children towards 'body awareness' and 'body thinking'.

These things take time and commitment, but in addressing them we will be helping children to take responsibility for more than just their own 'body thinking'. A well-structured, well-resourced programme which increases children's awareness of their bodies and stimulates their brains will have far-reaching consequences.

Dance depends on movement but all movement is not necessarily dance. Young children need opportunities for both. They need to see adults dancing, to dance with adults, to dance freely and expressively and to be supported in linking movement sequences together to form dances. When the time is right they need the opportunity to perform their dances to an audience of friendly and appreciative adults and peers. Settings must ensure that children can explore and practise movement for its own sake. They should be given opportunities to move in response to a wide variety of music and sounds, and learn about the ways in which movements can be combined creatively to produce a dance. Earlier we wrote about beat competence. Dance provides one of the most effective ways of feeling and expressing beat.

*Independent Learning in the Foundation Stage*

## Getting started with independence in music, movement and dance

- Ensure that children have repeated opportunities to hear music, live and recorded.
- Sing with and to the children. Dance with and for the children. Don't worry if you're not an expert – children are very forgiving and will really appreciate you joining in.
- Be enthusiastic in your response to children's singing, movement and dancing.
- Allow children time to build on what they have heard and seen modelled.
- Develop children's body and spatial (kinesthetic) intelligence by helping them to become aware of all the different ways in which their bodies will move and the ways space can be used.
- Look for ways of approaching other work through dance, for example by exploring the meaning of words through movement.
- Encourage children to use their own ideas in the composition of movement sequences and dances and to move with objects in various ways, e.g. hoops, balls, beanbags, lengths of materials and so on.
- Children need to make choices and decisions about which rhymes or songs will be sung, which instruments will be played, how loudly or softly sounds should be made or sung and the tempo at which a piece should be performed. Once they have gained experience of being in control they will gain the confidence to repeat experiences on their own.
- We need to ask ourselves whether we, as adults, have developed our own 'body thinking'.
- Incorporate music that the children listen to at home, by encouraging them to bring favourite recordings into your setting.

## Ideas for resources to support independence in music, movement and dance

- Set up a 'performance area' where children can go to perform musical pieces, movement sequences and dances – it could easily be outside.
- Supply a range of objects, fabrics and artefacts to support children's movement ideas, e.g. scarves, ribbon sticks, lengths of material, hoops, beanbags, etc.
- Buy a simple CD player and teach the children how to use it.
- Provide a big mirror so children can see themselves moving and dancing.
- Search out books and stories about dance, music and dancing.
- Keep a stock of simple musical instruments for children to access independently as well as for more organised music sessions.

- Encourage children to make their own sound effects for stories and play scenarios, using 'body sounds' and simple instruments.
- Have an outside basket for musical instruments.
- Try a simple microphone for Karaoke sessions.
- Use large pieces of lycra or other fabric for movement play.
- Make some simple 'home made' instruments, shakers, scrapers, plastic box drums etc.
- Explore the environment for sounds in nature or other objects.
- Sometimes use a radio or CD player to echo the music children hear at home.
- Collect examples of music that reflects local communities and cultures.
- Try offering a light source, such as a projector or OHP machine so the children can dance in the light.
- Use objects, instruments, artefacts and stories as starting points for music and movement.
- Talk about how the weather or the season makes us want to move – provide some resources that make the sounds of winter or windy weather.
- Diwali, Christmas, Chinese New Year and other festivals can offer resources to inspire movement and dance.

## Managing storage and access

- Musical instruments need care and upkeep. Teach children how to take care of them and use them properly.
- A music trolley is an ideal, but if you haven't got room or can't afford it, put the instruments in small baskets or boxes. If you line these with fabric, it will protect the instruments.
- Store your instruments in several places – near the outside door, in the book corner to accompany stories and songs, near your music centre or CD player.
- If you keep the instruments on shelves, draw their shapes on the shelves so children know where to return each instrument.
- Store CDs in transparent pockets or an 'over the door' shoe racks.

## A case study of encouraging independence in music, movement and dance

Supporting movement play and dance as a child-initiated activity takes sensitivity, as these activities should not lead to organised 'performances' any more than brick play or role-play do. In this setting there is a performance area where children can stage their creations if they wish, but

there is no pressure to do so, and children can access the area with or without others to watch.

The children had been inspired by a dance session lead by Mrs Patel. She had demonstrated a variety of dances from her culture and then worked with the children with long lengths of beautiful fabric. This session had been met with such enthusiasm that the other adults asked Mrs Patel if it would be possible to borrow the fabric so that they could use it again to build on the experience they had so much enjoyed.

As soon as it was time for child-initiated learning to begin a group of children hurried to the area, excitedly discussing their plans to 'do that dancing again!' Yasmin eagerly gave out the material while Thomas went to the CD player to start the music. Unfortunately, although Mrs Patel had been very willing to loan her fabric to the children she had needed to take the music away with her. Realising what had happened Thomas suggested that they try some other music, but after three or four alternatives the children all agreed that none of the music was suitable. 'Why don't we make up our own music?' said Omar. 'We could use the instruments!'

The music area was next to the 'performance area'. This had been a conscious decision on the part of the practitioners so that the work in both areas could overlap. Omar, Jack and Amy rushed over to the instruments and selected tambourines, a small snare drum and a 'rain stick'. After some exploration, and further negotiation about who would play what, the 'orchestra' enthusiastically began to play.

'You're playing too loud!' said Yasmin. 'We don't need it that loud!'

After several attempts and some support from an adult the noise level was gradually adjusted and the dancers began swaying, swirling and running with their lengths of fabric, weaving in and out in complex patterns. This continued for some time until Yasmin, who was emerging as a budding choreographer, began to suggest other ways in which the fabric could be manipulated by individuals and pairs of children, and the dance developed. All joined in except Omar, who insisted on doing his own thing, completely absorbed in watching the fabrics as they swirled above his head.

'Look, he's spoiling it,' said Jack. 'He won't do it right.'

With a little sensitive intervention from the adult, the problem was soon resolved and Omar's movement sequence became an extension of the dance. This resulted in other children wanting to do the same until the dance became quite long and the musicians returned to their previous volume.

'Its great,' exclaimed Yasmin. 'If we practised we could do it for everybody at circle time.' Everyone agreed that this was a good idea, and after several more rehearsals the children hurried away to the writing area to make invitations to their performance.

In this case study it is clear that the children had a great deal of control over what was going on. They were absorbed in the movement play and began to shape it themselves. This did need some support from an adult, but help was given in a sensitive way that supported the play, allowing space for individuals to become involved, while recognising their unique interests and needs.

## Suggestions for giving your children ownership of dance and movement play

- Organise and equip your setting just as carefully for movement play as you would for any other activity.
- Move with children, modelling creativity and confidence.
- Notice and observe children moving, commenting on what you see.
- Create situations and plan activities that focus on movement, sensation and feelings, and use the language of movement.
- Support children in taking the lead in movement activities. Encourage them to compose their own pieces, movement sequences and dances. Look for something to value in every effort.
- Play a wide variety of music and encourage children to talk about their favourites and why they like them.
- Compose 'sound pictures' – let the children decide the subject – zoo, park, seaside, forest, etc. – and encourage them to discuss various ways of making the sounds. Make up songs, rhymes and jingles. Set up a music area where children can use instruments and make music throughout the daily routine.
- Let children take the lead when composing music pieces and dances.
- Arrange for the children to hear adults and older children singing, playing instruments and dancing.
- Make collections of different things that children can move with, and let them decide the 'what, with and how' for the movement session.

## Questions to ask when you review the quality of music and movement play in your setting

- How much do you value music, dance and movement play? How effectively do you support the development of 'body intelligence?'
- Are there enough opportunities for children to compose their own music, sound sequences and dances? Are there enough opportunities for children to perform music and dance?
- Are the children able to watch others perform? (Children learn by listening, watching and copying)
- Is there enough space for children to play instruments and move freely, without disturbing others? Have the children been taught how to care for the resources?

# Chapter 14:
# Creativity and critical thinking

There is no doubt that creative development has a real impact on self esteem and achievement; both observation and research confirm this. It is essential for all of us who work with children, and especially those in early years settings, to help children realise that they are creative beings. But first we need to think about how we help children to develop their creativity. This should involve the whole team in understanding the creative process as it needs not only thought, but time for thought, and time to plan worthwhile opportunities which will stimulate the growth of children's creative capacities.

It is useful to begin by brainstorming ideas about what creativity means in your setting. You may like to compare your ideas with those of Bernadette Duffy, who has done a great deal of research into this issue. She presents her conclusions with great skill in her book *Supporting Creativity and Imagination in the Early Years*. Creativity, she says, depends on the ability to see things in fresh ways. It involves learning from past experiences and relating this learning to new situations, as well as thinking along unorthodox lines and breaking barriers. Creative thinkers will use non-traditional approaches to solving problems, going further than the information given, and that will lead to the creation of something unique or original.

Most people find that their ideas about creativity match this definition pretty closely, but where do we go from here? We need to think about what is involved in helping children to acquire these capabilities. What opportunities and experiences should be provided? It is all very well to have creative ideas but unless we have the skills and abilities to realise them, they will amount to little. We need to help children develop the attitudes and dispositions to make the most of their creative ideas and impulses, the persistence to keep going when things don't work out straight away. We also need to make allowances – creativity can be a messy process and sometimes, as adults, our attempts to make it less messy inhibit children's independence of both thought and action.

> Creativity and critical thinking are processes that are child led, but which benefit greatly from the sensitive contributions of others. The processes involve making connections between things, people or places in ways that are new and personally meaningful.
>
> *Effective practice: Creativity and Critical Thinking; EYFS pack; CD Rom; DCSF; 2008*

## Links with key early Learning Goals

*Creative development*

- Explore colour, texture, shape, form and space in two and three dimensions
- Respond in a variety of ways to what they see, hear, smell, touch, feel
- Express and communicate their ideas, thoughts and feelings by using a widening range of materials and suitable tools.

A well-resourced creative area offers children a challenging and exciting context in which to develop the skills of independent learning. The creative area should be ideally situated near to a water supply and there should be a suitable floor surface and space for several children to work. Where possible children should be able to choose whether to work at a table, an easel or on the floor. They should also be able to work outside, for example by attaching paper to walls and fences, or to put it on the floor. There should be a wide range of media and equipment, readily available.

As well as physical space we need to make space in the daily routine to facilitate the development of creativity. We must be flexible enough to allow children to continue working on something in which they are deeply involved, even though we might have planned for something else. We should also try to ensure that there are opportunities for children to see other people painting, modelling and creating. This does not have to be professional artists; older children, practitioners and other adults can all provide valuable role models. We need to make time for children to be involved in the display of their own work, although this often takes longer than putting it up ourselves. And we need to provide time for children to share work with others, describe what they have done and talk about the processes they went through.

Supporting the creative development of children is one of the most difficult and subtle aspects of the work of early years practitioners. Children need sensitive and focused help to develop the skills to reach their goals. Often children know what they want to create but do not know how to achieve it. If we do not address this it can lead to frustration and stifle creative expression.

One way to help is for adults to demonstrate new materials, equipment and techniques and to draw, paint and model alongside the children. Above all, adults should openly value children's creative expressions, especially when they are being displayed. Adults can also help by supporting children in taking risks and experimenting, and by making sure that there are opportunities for children to co-operate and collaborate on projects. It is also the role of adults to broaden children's minds and stimulate their imaginations by introducing them to art from cultures other than their own.

## Getting started with independence in creativity and critical thinking

- Share the work of famous artists with the children – you can get reproductions and posters from 'budget' bookshops. Ask the children, 'How do you think the artist did this?'
- Borrow objects from your local museum and encourage the children to describe what they see, think about how it was made and talk about whether they like it and why.
- Make sure that the book corner or library contains books about famous artists.
- Arrange for the children to visit local galleries – ask if they will consider putting on a special exhibition for young children.
- Put together a display of paintings that use different media. Encourage the children to notice and talk about the different ways in which the artists have worked
- Make displays of photographs and discuss the ways in which they have been taken (e.g. viewpoint, light, colours, etc.).
- Collect postcards and greeting cards with paintings and photos. Put these in a scrapbook or a photo display book.
- Use photos of details of your setting and garden to start conversations about colours, shapes and textures.

## Ideas for resources to support independence in creativity

- Make a collection of different tools for applying paint – brushes, sticks, brooms with soft bristles, squeezy bottles, sprays and cotton buds.
- Tools for clay, dough and other malleable materials should include sticks, clay tools, blunt knives, cutters, rolling pins, cake trays, sieves and graters, eggcups and other small containers.
- Add some more unusual tools such as household objects (spoons, sieves, cutlery or potato mashers) or cooking tools (icing bags, cake tins, wooden spoons, whisks).
- Offer hole punches, staplers and plenty of white glue for collage and for decorating creations.
- Don't forget that fingers, hands and feet can also be creative tools. Provide plenty of opportunities to use these free and tactile tools. Experiment and talk about the different possibilities and effects.
- Photograph children's projects at various stages of development for display. Help them to recall and discuss the process.
- Make sure you offer different sizes of brushes, paint pots, mark makers.

*Creativity and critical thinking*

- Don't forget that creativity isn't just painting – offer dough, clay, foam, ice, collage, fabric work, string, thread and ribbon.
- Children need opportunities to work very big or very small, so provide big sheets of card and fabric, tubes and boxes as well as very small items such as sequins and glitter, buttons, straws and small pasta shapes, lentils or rice.
- Working out of doors gives a whole new range of freedom. Offer painting on fences and sheds, creating dens from painted sheets or shower curtains and decorating boxes or crates.
- Use natural materials for creative work – leaves, bark, mud, sawdust and wood shavings, twigs and nuts; stones and pebbles; seeds and seed heads.
- Encourage collaboration in big paintings and other creations such as tie-dye, collages, chalk on paths, paper pinned to tree trunks etc.
- Offer date stamps and name stickers so children can label their own work.

## Managing storage and access

- Allocate some space for work in progress, for work to dry, and for ongoing projects to be left out for completion later. Aprons, sinks and brooms should be accessible and the children should be encouraged to take responsibility for themselves and their surroundings.
- Materials should be accessible and stored at the right height. Children should be able to call on a range of paper in various weights, colours and sizes, carefully stored so that they can make decisions and choices about what they would like to use.
- Sometimes, if not all the time, they should be able to mix their own paint.
- Store creative material for outdoor work in trolleys or baskets, easy to transport to the garden.
- Flat storage for wet paintings makes them easier to manage.

## A case study of encouraging independence in creativity

Children's work is unique and individual. Colouring a picture that someone else has drawn or creating identical cards involves little creativity or independence. It is what the individual child contributes that matters. We should always keep in mind that the process of creating has more value than the finished product. Consider what the children are experiencing in this setting.

Jessie was fascinated when Adina, her key person, brought some of her own watercolours to show the children, and the picture of Adina's garden was her favourite.

The following day, Jessie said she was going to make a picture of her own garden, and began to talk excitedly about the things she wanted to include. Jessie set to work,

*Independent Learning in the Foundation Stage*

and for a period of time became so engrossed in exploring the effects of the paint that she almost forgot about her intention to paint her garden. As Adina observed she sensitively allowed Jessie to experiment with the paint, watching as she washed over the entire piece of paper with a mix of colours. When this was complete, Adina asked her about the things that were in her garden and how she wanted to represent them.

'I want to do my swing and my slide, and the tree, and all the flowers,' said Jessie. 'We've got lots and lots of flowers.'

After thinking carefully for a moment or two, Jessie selected a medium sized brush and fetched a pot of black paint. Jessie was now interested in the bold lines of her swing and her slide, which she painted with great care. When she realised that there was no green paint she carefully spooned some green powder paint into a pot, added water and mixed until the paint was the colour and texture she needed.

Her next step was to make the flowers. She went to the collage table and collected some art straws and some shiny coloured paper, and collected some scissors to make the flowers. She placed the finished flowers on top of the painting, expecting them to stick to the paint. Adina watched with interest when, having written her name on a label and stuck it on her picture, Jessie began to carry her finished piece of work to the drying rack.

'Oh no!' she cried, as all her carefully cut flowers fell to the floor. Adina helped her to pick up the pieces.

'How do you think we could stop all your flowers falling off?' prompted Adina.

'I think I need to glue them,' said Jessie.

'You go and get the glue then,' suggested Adina, 'and I'll finish picking up your flowers.

When the picture was complete Jessie said 'I like my picture!'

'So do I!' said Adina.

'There,' said Jessie, 'Now I can put it to dry. The flowers are all stuck now.'

With great satisfaction Jessie took her completed picture to dry.

Jessie knew what she wanted to do and was clearly in control of the creative process. She was able to call on Adina when she needed technical help, and Adina was available to support at crucial points, helping without taking over, and leaving the decisions to Jessie.

## Suggestions for giving your children ownership of creative work and thinking

- Show them what materials will do and then stand back and allow them to use them in their own way.
- Respect their ideas, even when they conflict with what you would most like e.g. the child who paints a lovely picture and then wants to cover the whole thing with black paint. He may really need to do this!
- Involve them in setting up the creative area. Start by asking questions like, 'What materials would you most like to work with today?' Let the

children cover the surfaces, get the materials ready, mix the paint, make the dough.

- If possible, let them decide where they would like to draw, paint or model. Painting outside will provide a very different experience from painting inside and will trigger some different ideas.
- Provide spaces where children can display their own two and three-dimensional representations. Ask them where and how they would most like to display their work.
- Involve children in selecting and ordering resources and equipment for the creative area. They love to look through the catalogues and it helps them to understand that we cannot always have everything we would like.
- Train the children to use a camera so that they can record the progress of their projects at their various stages.
- Make sure some of your display space is at children's eye level and an easy height for them to both display and look closely at their own and others' work.

### Questions to ask when you review the quality of creativity and critical thinking in your setting

- How do you plan for children's creative experiences? Do your plans focus on outcomes or processes?
- How sensitive are you when you interact with children in the creative area? Do you 'tune-in' to what they want to explore, listen carefully to ascertain their purpose and support them in achieving their goals (even when they are different from yours)?
- Have you worked with parents and carers to help them understand the importance of process over outcome? It must be extremely distressing for a child who has worked hard on a particular creation to be greeted apathetically with, 'And what's that supposed to be?'
- Do the children have access to a wide range of resources and media? Could you involve the children more in decisions about which materials they would most like to work with and the ways in which they would like to use them?
- Do you know enough about the ways in which children develop creativity? Does the staff team have the fullest possible understanding of creativity as a life-enhancing process which is crucially important to people's lives? Has the team explored the links between creativity and achievement?

*Independent Learning in the Foundation Stage*

# Chapter 15:
# Messy activities

'Messy' activities are an essential part of work in all early years settings. When children play with sand, water, malleable materials and wood, they learn skills, concepts, attitudes and approaches that are transferable to every other area of learning. In a well-planned setting children do this in a way that helps the development of their independence and their initiative. But this does not simply happen; it requires that the staff team give time and energy to ensuring that such opportunities are there.

When thinking about fostering children's independence in their approach to 'messy' and practical activities it is helpful to start by exploring how we feel about mess, and our own attitudes and anxieties. Without such introspection it is easy for us to inhibit, albeit unconsciously, children's opportunities to engage fully in such activities.

This is a particular danger if we have a rigid view of what a tidy room should look like. We need to ask ourselves to what extent our own notions of 'order and tidiness' govern what happens in the messy area. Are we afraid to really share control with the children in these aspects of learning because we are concerned about the potential for chaos? Do we observe the ways children use materials so that we can fully facilitate their learning, or are we more concerned about keeping things tidy? Are we worried about how our space will appear to premises officers, cleaners, parents?

The messy area can cause a lot of anxiety because of its potential for what might seem like chaos, and on a large scale. A tight rein on the children's actions will avoid this, but it will also inhibit exploration, experimentation and learning. In such a case we will probably spend most of our time going round after the children tidying up. Adults need to agree the difference between productive, creative mess, and an untidy shambles. While the former is stimulating and exciting the latter is no use to anybody and gets in the way of learning. So they should agree the point at which materials become too untidy. The main criterion has to be the point at which the play goes off track. When this

This sort of play is important because its lack of a focus on making or producing something leaves the child free to explore all sorts of possibilities. It taps into children's innate curiosity about the world around them and their strong desire to explore and find out more.

*Bernadette Duffy; Effective practice: Messy Play; EYFS pack; CD Rom; DCSF; 2008*

happens no-one will be able to play productively until the resources have been sorted out and a measure of order restored.

It often helps if we can shunt some of the messy activities out of doors. We need to consider how effectively we make use of the outdoor area for messy play, and ensure that we make the most of the opportunities offered.

## Links with key early Learning Goals

Messy activities can be used to develop every area of learning but some of the major goals are:

*Personal, social & emotional development*
- continue to be interested, excited & motivated to learn
- be confident to try new ideas and activities
- work as part of a group or class, taking turns and sharing fairly

*Knowledge and understanding of the world*
- investigate objects and materials by using all of their senses as appropriate
- find out about, and identify some features of, living things, objects and events they observe
- look closely at similarities, differences, patterns and change
- ask questions about why things happen and how they work
- build and construct with a wide range of objects, selecting appropriate resources, and adapting their work where necessary
- select the tools and techniques they need to shape, assemble, and join the materials they are using

*Creative development*
- explore colour, shape, texture, form and space in two and three dimensions

This sort of work naturally throws up issues to do with children's safety and wellbeing. We all have the safety of children foremost in our hearts, as well as having a duty of care to those in our charge. Moreover, we live in an increasingly litigious society where fears about legal action have prompted us to be cautious about children taking risks. Activities such as woodwork can cause anxieties, but many of these are lessened when the staff team agree what children may do and how they may do it. For example, certain activities require a minimum level of staffing. There will be occasions when we may not be able to guarantee that, so we need some way of making it clear to the children that these activities are off the menu. While the wellbeing of the children is paramount, we have to ask ourselves the extent to which our natural anxiety for their health and safety is impoverishing their learning.

One harassed practitioner we encountered was at her wits end because day after day every single thing was taken out and put into the sand and water

tray. The result was that there was so much out that no-one could play effectively with anything. The way to help her was to 'scaffold' the decision-making process. In other words, she had to get the children to understand that the decisions they made had implications for themselves and everyone else wanting to play in the messy area. It was not at first easy to do this. To begin with, the children argued over the resources and tried to stake their claim on a corner of the sand tray or particular equipment, but by setting up a structure and opportunities for the children to talk through their problems and feelings, to become aware of the needs and wishes of others and to plan their use of resources, she helped them grow in confidence and independence without stifling their spontaneity or creativity. She had given the control to them.

Practitioners need to think laterally. Some of the most productive play with sand, water, malleable materials and wood happens when practitioners use their creative impulses and introduce unusual materials into the area. Once children have seen the new possibilities these offer, their imaginations are fired and they can go on to use these things in their own way.

## Getting started with independence in messy play

- Link messy, creative play with stories e.g. *Where the Wild Things Are*; *The Rainbow Fish* and traditional tales such as *The Three Little Pigs* and *Little Red Riding Hood*. The children will extend their language, imagination and creativity by using models and figures in the sand and water, and building habitats and scenes to fit the storylines.
- Negotiate boundaries within which play from the different areas can overlap e.g. constructions made in the woodwork area can be used in the sand and water, or figures made with clay or dough incorporated into other aspects of play.
- Spend time observing the ways in which children are using the materials. This will enable you to 'fine-tune' the management of space, add appropriate materials and ensure that you make meaningful interactions which will facilitate purposeful play.
- Ensure that children have the appropriate protective clothing for the task in hand e.g. appropriate waterproof garments in the water area, protective goggles in the woodwork area.
- Enable children to use resources from other areas with the sand, water and malleable materials e.g. models and figures from the 'small world' area can give real life and vigour to the play in these areas.
- Be clear with the children which resources may be used, which may not, and why. This could be as simple as covering the woodwork table with a drape, or displaying a symbol that conveys the same message, and empowers them to make appropriate choices.

- Provide a wide range of resources for children to use in sand, water, dough etc. These should be stored where children can select them.
- Bury some 'treasure' in the sand for the children to discover e.g. some old coins in a small treasure box, or a bundle of old keys.
- Encourage children to experiment with the tools and resources they use.

## Ideas for resources to support independence in messy play

- Make simple recipe cards so children can make their own dough.
- Encourage children to use all sorts of tools and surfaces to mark and shape their creations.
- Provide some natural materials, such as leaves, twigs or seeds to incorporate in these creative experiences.
- Remember that cooking is a malleable activity. Provide plenty of opportunities for children to get involved in simple cookery.
- Offer cooking utensils for malleable play – saucepans, bun tins, whisks, scoops, rolling pins and cutters.
- Try some more unusual tactile materials – jelly, cooked spaghetti, ice, snow, custard, shaving foam etc.
- Collect and display posters in the sand, water, dough and woodwork areas that promote discussion and give the children ideas for things they could try out.
- Add smells, textures and sparkle to dough by using glitter, sequins, rice, colour, etc.
- Use different things in the sand and water trays, e.g. noodles (cooked or uncooked), spaghetti, bark, compost, pebbles, gravel, lentils, slime, porridge, etc.
- Offer small buckets and lengths of hosepipe so that children can fill and empty water trays for themselves.
- Create unusual and exciting opportunities for children to handle different materials e.g. ice sculptures (freeze water overnight in large plastic containers, provide the children with mittens and 'safety' goggles and see what can be produced using small chisels and pounding tools).
- Find some appropriate information books and display them in these areas.
- Add unusual things to the water tray e.g. ice cubes with sequins or flowers frozen in them.
- Introduce and model new materials and tools so children can make choices and decisions with plenty of information.
- Put a 'cooker' and a range of cooking utensils close to the modelling area, as much of the work with dough and clay involves food.
- Make sure children have suitable, small sized dustpans, brushes and brooms for clearing up.

## Managing storage and access

- Store basic materials for sand, water, modelling and woodwork so that they are easily accessible to the children. Additional materials should be kept in labelled boxes.
- The labels should be appropriate for the children's stage of development. Make use of pictures and colours. But be prepared, children will want to mix and match the resources, and this may drive a coach and horses through your carefully organised storage system.
- Provide well organised hanging space for aprons and protective clothing. Aprons with front fastenings are easier for children to put on and do up for themselves.
- Provide clearly labelled baskets and boxes of additional materials and tools for sand and water play, and a good range of safe and well organised materials for working with wood i.e. offcuts that have been appropriately sanded to minimise the risk of splinters.
- Show children how to use tools and demonstrate how tools should be carried. Real tools are better and safer in the end than blunt 'pretend' versions – blunt saws can be wielded with so much force in an attempt to get a job done that children can easily lose their hold and hurt themselves. Decide if there are any tools that are just for the use of adults and if there are, give children your reasons for restricting them.

## A case study of encouraging independence in messy play

Consider this account of some work in a setting and think about its strengths. Creative thinkers are sometimes difficult to incorporate in a well-organised setting, but their needs are great and we should be prepared to be flexible in our responses, and prepared to change our plans in the interests of the children's learning.

Some of the children were really enjoying being involved in digging in the nursery garden. As the children dug they discovered some smooth, white, round stones. They were fascinated by these and spent a long time handling them, until one of them suggested that they might be dinosaur eggs.

Adam, said that it would be a good idea to bury the eggs in the sand so that they could hatch. He collected the stones together and made off for the sand tray where they buried them all.

'Why don't we put some dinosaurs in?' suggested Trevor, and he headed off, returning with a box of plastic dinosaurs. For the next few minutes the small group of children became engrossed in arranging the dinosaurs in the sand tray.

The children decided that they needed some trees for the dinosaurs, and they thought they would probably be able to find some in the garden, so Mrs Turner, one

of the adults, fetched the secateurs and they all headed outside. The children selected the foliage that they needed to make trees in the sand tray and hurried back inside to put them in place. This was easier said than done as the foliage kept toppling over in the dry sand.

'We need to wet the sand to make them stand up right!' announced Sarah, and she picked up a bucket and hurried over to the sink. After much wetting and patting the sand the foliage stood up and the children seemed pleased with the results.

Adam had been to the book corner to fetch a book about dinosaurs. When he returned he had the book open at the middle page where there was a stunning dinosaur picture. 'Look,' he said, 'We need some stones, there's lots of rocks in this picture!'

'We could get them from outside,' suggested Trevor, and once again everyone went back outside for a stone hunt. Large, muddy, lumpy stones were collected and the children washed them in the sink. Eva filled the sink with water and the stones were soon cleaned and ready to be added to the diorama in the sand tray. Adam wanted to make some pterodactyls.

'How, though?' asked Sarah.

'We could do them out of clay,' said Amy.

The children searched out Mrs Turner to ask if they could have some clay, and before long were busy fashioning their own dinosaurs. As soon as these were made, they carried them to the sand tray

In this example we have emphasised the need for the adults to let go, to give children their heads – in this area of learning perhaps more than any other. The case study illustrates how this ownership can energise children and unlock their creative potential. Think how much more the children have learnt here, with Mrs Turner as a sensitive observer and facilitator, than if they had simply been instructed and given materials to make a dinosaur scene.

## Suggestions for giving your children ownership of creative, messy play

- Invite visitors to talk about their work e.g. potters, carpenters, cooks, etc. (they don't have to be professionals).
- Use stories, objects and characters to inspire creative play.
- Refer children's ideas to other children so that they can gain inspiration from each other.
- Instead of putting out resources for the children ask, 'What do you plan to do in the sand/water/modelling area/etc. today? What things do you think you will need?' Involve the children in choosing and ordering new equipment.

*Independent Learning in the Foundation Stage*

- Tune into what children are currently interested in and reflect these interests in the resources and materials you provide and the discussions you initiate.
- Have 'themed' boxes for sand and water play. Talk with the children about what they think should go in the boxes.
- Let the children take responsibility for filling and emptying the water tray.
- Allow the children to mix their own dough and decide what colour, texture or smell they would like it to have.
- Train them to use a camera so that they can photograph projects that have gone particularly well.
- Observe and note the conversations going between children. Use these as starting points for discussions, new resources and changes.

## Questions to ask when you review the quality of messy play in your setting

- As a staff team, have you spent time looking at how you will ensure safe, enjoyable play within these aspects? (N.B. A useful publication that will help you to do this is *Too Safe for their Own Good: helping children learn about risk and life skills* by Jennie Lindon, published by the National Early Years Network.)
- Have you talked about mess versus tidiness, so that you are all more or less in agreement about what is acceptable and what is not? Can you all tell the difference between creative and uncreative mess?
- Could you be more imaginative in the way you provide for these aspects of learning? Are there enough opportunities for children to pursue these activities outside?
- Do you give boys and girls equal stimulus and opportunity to participate in these aspects of work? Have you monitored this to find out?
- Do you encourage parents and children to contribute ideas, experiences, resources and expertise

We regard the creative area as one of the most important. Creative children have the motivation, independence of mind, attitudes and skills which enable them to shape their own learning.

When children have opportunities to play with ideas in different situations and with a variety of resources, they discover connections and come to new and better understandings and ways of doing things. Adult support in this process enhances their ability to think critically and ask questions.

*EYFS Principles into Practice cards 'The Learning Environment 'Creative Development''; DCSF; 2008*

# Chapter 16:
# Systems, structures and organisation

The aspects of the curriculum discussed so far in this section are concerned with specific activities and resources. This chapter addresses some of the systems and structures within a early years setting which will facilitate and aid the sorts of learning experiences we have discussed and described. These systems must be adapted to suit the age and stage of development of individuals and groups. How well they work will have a profound influence on children's developing independence and autonomy. Please be aware, in reading this chapter, of the needs of your setting and the children who attend it. We hope that some of the suggestions will be appropriate for you, while recognising that others may not.

### Helping children to organise themselves and take care of their personal belongings

This is a constant concern for practitioners, parents and the children themselves. Parents' anxiety is shown in the way they take over from them, doing things for them that, given a little time and space, children could do perfectly well for themselves – fetching coats, organising bags, looking for lost items of clothing and so on. The anxiety of practitioners often results in banning the bringing of things from home, lining children up to check their clothing or for clean hands, restricting free access to materials or space. Children display anxiety by standing helplessly while adults organise them, or by hanging on ferociously to tokens from home so they don't get lost, or by angrily saying, 'I can do that, don't rush me!'

Here are some suggestions for helping children to organise themselves – and us:

- Check the height of door handles and the ease of opening of the doors. Children must be safe, but they shouldn't feel trapped.
- Make sure the pegs are at child height and far enough apart for children to manage. Space around a peg will improve access and tidiness, particularly for winter clothes. Bigger hooks make for ease of

use. A shelf underneath serves as storage and a perch for changing shoes.

- Have a sewing session for parents and put a tape for hanging in each child's coat. Write the child's name on it before you sew it in.
- Label pegs and drawers with photos of the children. A digital camera makes this easier.
- Write names on clothes pegs, so shoes and wellies can stay together.
- A simple cloth bag hanging on each peg will accommodate small belongings such as gloves and hats. Let the children personalise them with fabric crayons.
- A low shelf and some name labels will ensure safety for toys and other treasures brought from home.
- A box just inside the door is useful for jumpers and other clothes removed in the garden.

## Supporting children's developing sense of self image and identity

This is another important area of early years work. Here are some ideas:

- Set up self registration with Velcro cards, pockets or boxes. Have photos as well as names to convey identity. Make some for staff as well.
- Photo boards and books with pictures of each child, their family and friends are sources of endless interest. Add some photos of children's homes, pets, etc.
- Take the children out and let them take pictures of the community and local places of social and cultural interest.
- Children love sending and receiving messages and letters. Make some message boxes from shoe boxes, and provide a message writing table.
- Use names and/or photos to identify individual cups and other personal articles.
- Involve the children in deciding the rules for play, what is fair and what is reasonable.

The bathrooms and toilets should be well-organised, pleasant places. Check towels, toilet paper and taps to ensure that they are easy to use and in the right place. Mirrors, flowers and plants make a lot of difference, and a chair or stool helps the place to look more homely.

Children can also be involved in planning and organising their own day and week. Of course, they need the opportunity to practise this and to realise that planning is a support, not a strait jacket. In order to do this, children need:

- uninterrupted time to engage in self-chosen activities.
- support from adults as they plan and organise their activities.
- easy access to equipment and materials.
- stability in the routine of the day and the location of equipment.
- easy ways of recording what they are going to do, in pictures, symbols and charts.
- recognition and praise for taking responsibility for their own activities.

If they have these things they can:

- decide what to do for at least part of the day.
- choose when (and where) to have snacks and drinks, and contribute to their organisation and content.
- think about tomorrow at the end of today.
- use charts, pictures with Velcro on the back, stickers or stamps to plan out their day.
- decide who to play with.
- make choices about joining group times.
- flow freely between indoors and the outdoors.
- help to plan trips, visits and outings.
- comment on the organisation of the setting.
- contribute to systems of rules, rewards and sanctions.
- have more input into when and how adult involvement would be helpful.

## Setting out and clearing up

Children can also be better involved in setting out and clearing up if they have more ownership of their activities. They see the importance of good organisation, they know where things are stored, they have an increased sense of responsibility for the equipment. Children could:

- help with the labelling and organisation of the room and the outside area.
- make suggestions about combinations of different sorts of materials.
- contribute to choosing new equipment and resources by looking at catalogues and visiting shops.
- label and caption their own models, pictures, constructions.
- decide whether and when they want to dismantle a project or construction – whether they have 'finished with it'.
- contribute to discussions about what went well and what worked.
- talk about what they learned and achieved during an activity.
- recognise the success of planning their own programme and the achievements of others.

*Independent Learning in the Foundation Stage*

- make their own 'record of achievement' and collections of work.
- take photos, make labels and displays, give demonstrations, invite visitors, record their own commentaries, explanations, directions either alone or with the help of other children or adults.

## Checklist

When examining your systems and structures it's useful to have a checklist, and this one might help. Are there:

- opportunities to work inside and out?
- opportunities to work alone and with others?
- areas for reflection and contemplation?
- places to write and read?
- places to leave work that is unfinished?
- tidy, well-organised spaces for storing resources?
- opportunities to combine materials in new and creative ways?
- opportunities to extend and complement activities outside?
- places for display? Plants, pictures and artefacts to interest them, and do they reflect local cultures?
- child-friendly furnishings and furniture?

Finally, are resources accessible? At the right height? Visible? Well labelled? In cupboards or drawers that are easy to reach and open? Safe for children to use?

Our original draft of this section offered readers an apology for its length. Now we are less inclined to make excuses! We feel that here is the kernel of what we are trying to achieve in this book. The philosophy, psychology and history of child development are very important. Case studies and accounts of practice elsewhere can provide useful ideas and pointers. But it is the actual, practical, day-to-day experiences of children in their settings which will enable and empower them as independent thinkers and set them on the way towards becoming confident, competent and successful learners. We hope you will find our advice useful, either by confirming the value of what you do already or suggesting some new ideas you could try – or perhaps a little of both.

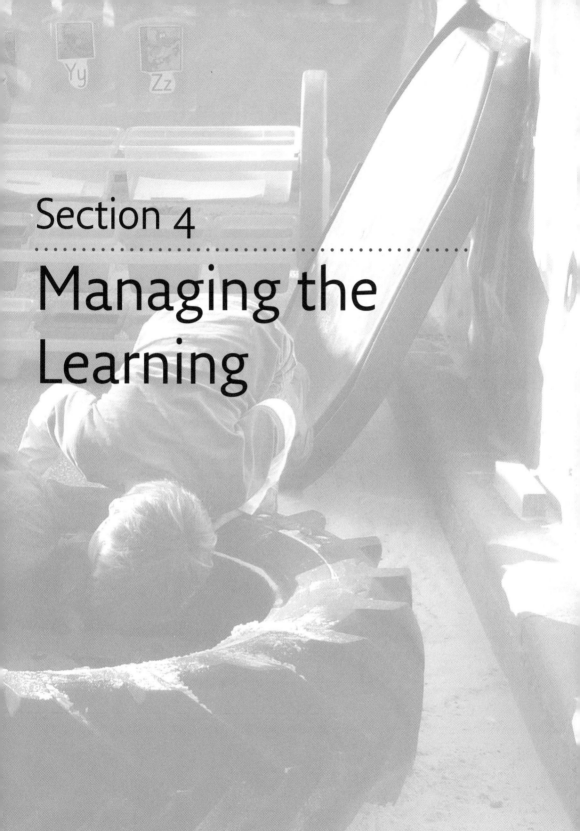

# Section 4

## Managing the Learning

# Chapter 17:
# Identifying excellence

It is always helpful to review what other people in other places are doing. In this chapter, we describe two of the most powerful, innovative and child-centred international models of excellence in early years education. Each of them has been established for many years, and each has developed its own features which have been evolved over time. Both systems have been scrutinised, celebrated, criticised and held up as examples. Both have been proved to have a lifelong effect on children and their families. Both have been emulated elsewhere, and have influenced the practice of the many visitors, trainees and thoughtful practitioners all over the world who have encountered their work.

The two models have many similarities, and as you read about them we hope you will recognise many of the features, practices and principles which underpin this book. We, as authors, owe debts to the adults and children who have shared their practice and knowledge with us through books, training and personally in their settings. They have been our guides and inspiration as we try to identify the next steps in providing an education which truly meets the needs of our 21st century children.

## Reggio Emilia, Italy. Pre-schools and infant and toddler centres

The city of Reggio is in the north of Italy, between Milan and Bologna on the plain of the river Po. It is the largest and richest region in the country. It is a region where people work hard, in the cities and on the land, and where often both parents in a family are employed. The city is proud of the fact that the Italian flag, the tricolor, was born there in 1797. Reggio is a middle-sized city, with about 130,000 inhabitants (roughly the same size as, say, Swindon). It has a cathedral and many churches, two theatres, a bell tower, a myriad

*Independent Learning in the Foundation Stage*

of squares, parks and fountains, museums, a fantastic market and a rather humid climate, sometimes oppressive in the heat of summer and often foggy and wet in the autumn, winter and spring. It is an agricultural region, and you can eat local Parmesan cheese and Parma Ham and drink Lambrusco or an espresso while you watch the world go by from the many local bars and restaurants.

## How did it start?

The first Reggio pre-school was set up six days after the end of the Second World War, in the spring of 1945. Italy had suffered badly in the later stages of the war, and the education system was in poor shape. All the schools were provided by the church, but with hardly any money in many places there was no school available for young children. Moreover, the education available at church schools was often very traditional and academic.

Desperate about the situation in their village, a group of mothers founded and built a school to serve their small community of Via Cella, just north of the city of Reggio. They paid for the materials they needed by selling a tank, some trucks and some horses left behind by the retreating German army. Loris Malaguzzi, a young teacher, heard what they were doing and offered his services as adviser, volunteer and friend. Malaguzzi worked with the Reggio schools throughout his life, and over the next 30 years developed into a powerful and influential educational thinker.

The first school soon inspired others, not only built but organised, funded and run by parents. They had little money, so they used abandoned or donated buildings, local volunteers and home-made or improvised equipment – very much like our volunteer playgroups. Most of these schools survived and thrived until the 1960s, when the first municipal school was built. This was the first secular municipal school for young children in Italy, and broke the monopoly of the Catholic church in early education. Since the 1960s many of the original schools have been incorporated into the municipal system, and the group of settings now comprises:

What is relatively simple, new work with young children is about to require teachers to rethink and change their assumptions about and expectations of children, their way of organising time and their style of working, and their way of developing curriculum and planning their days and activities. It required them to develop new skills and take risks, to give extra time, to collaborate, and to critique each other. None of these changes is simple. After four years we are still struggling with some aspects of all of them.

*Louise Boyd Cadwell, Bringing Reggio Emilia Home; Teachers College Press; 1997*

25 preschools
27 infant-toddler centers
540 staff (teaching and other)
45 school buildings.

A vast network of services which since 2004 has made it possible to create opportunity for every family requesting a place. In Reggio Emilia thanks to the existence of communal, state and private facilities about 1,600 children attend infant-toddler centers and represent 40% of children in the 0–3 age group (this is one of the highest percentages in Italy). About 90% of children in the corresponding age group attend preschools (about 4,600 children).

*Reggio Children; Zerosei; 2008*

These schools grew out of their local communities, and have always worked at their heart. The children are encouraged to feel part of the community. They use the local area as a resource for learning, and make frequent visits into the city and the surrounding country. Parents are still highly involved in their children's learning. Regular meetings, briefings, written and verbal communications enrich this involvement – impressive, considering that a majority of the parents are both in employment.

Among the most striking things about the children in these schools are their confidence and maturity. They assume control, responsibility and planning naturally because that is what they expect. They respect and work well with each other, and draw freely on the skills of the adults around them, seeking advice or help when they feel it is needed, asking for opinions and evaluations. The schools are constantly visited by practitioners, learning experts and government officers from all over the world. An exhibition featuring the work of some of the children, called 'The Hundred Languages of Children', has been touring the world for many years, and a new research centre was built and opened in Reggio to accommodate the huge number of practitioners wishing to visit and study the Reggio philosophy.

There some clear concepts on which the Reggio schools base their practice. They are foundation principles which have been confirmed and developed over the years, and have been set out by Louise Boyd Caldwell in *Bringing Reggio Emilia Home*. Many of these principles are central features in this book:

**The child as protagonist**, an active force in his or her own learning. Children are strong, rich and capable. They are the third protagonist, with their teachers and parents, and their rights are equal to those of the others (see Chapter 4).

**The child as collaborator with others**. Each child is in a collaborative

relationship with other children, family, teachers and the community (see the case studies in Section 3).

**The child as communicator**. Reggio schools have a systematic focus on words, movement, drawing, painting, building, sculpture, shadow play, dramatic play, collage and music. Children have the right to use any materials in order to discover and communicate what they know, understand, wonder about, question, feel and imagine, 'making their thinking visible' (Chapters 5 and 6).

**The environment as third teacher**. The child's needs are central in the design and use of space (Chapters 6 and 7).

**The teacher as partner, nurturer and guide**, facilitating children's exploration of themes, work on short and long projects and guiding experiences of joint, open-ended discovery and problem solving. Teachers listen to and observe children closely, asking questions, aiding discovery, feeding children's words and thoughts back to them to enable them to pursue their thinking (Chapter 5).

**The teacher as researcher**. Teachers work in pairs and maintain a strong collegiate relationship with all other teachers and staff, engaging in continuous discussion and interpretation of their work and the work of the children. They document their work and the work of the children, charting the progress of projects, individuals and child development in general.

**Documentation as communication**. Careful consideration and attention is given to the work of children and adults, and commentaries, transcriptions and photographs, composed into panels, books and displays are a feature of the schools. These also form an archive of the work of the school, kept centrally to act as a record of the work of the system as a whole (see Section 3).

**The parents as partners**. Parents play an essential role in the work of the schools, not as adjuncts or interferers but as full partners.

## What you might see in a Reggio School

The following account is based on visits to the Diana School, and on meetings, discussions and correspondence with some of the teachers. Although every school in the Reggio group differs slightly, the environment, ethos and organisation of the Diana School are typical.

The school is in a municipal park, within easy walking distance of the city centre, the piazzas, churches and shops. It is surrounded by trees and grass, and once through the security gate, the front entrance is open and

welcoming. The doors and walls have glass panels and big windows, so you can see both in and out. The foyer has welcoming notices, children's pictures, photos of children and staff.

Children arrive any time between 7:30am (for many of them have parents who must be at work by eight) and 9:00am, by which time all children are expected to be present. Parents and other carers come into the school as they bring their children, to talk with the teachers and to look at the children's work and the displays. During this first period, children are free to choose what they do, with whom and where. Small groups of friends may spend time in the piazza (a central indoor area onto which other rooms open), dressing up, reading, playing or just chatting. Others collect games and toys from shelves and cupboards. Some children sit with friends and teachers, planning what they will do during the day, sharing family news and activities.

By 9:00am all the children are present and the class groups meet in their own rooms to share news and plan the day. The teachers (two in each room) introduce the planned activities, and talk with the children about what happened the day before, reminding them of what they did, suggesting to individuals and groups how they might continue with projects or develop new aspects and ideas. Sometimes the teachers will include work from the previous day and talk about this, inviting comments and questions from the children; at other times they may play a recording or read from a transcript of the children's words.

Projects are undertaken by groups, or, more rarely, by the whole class. The membership and size of groups may change over time as the project they are working on develops. Children and teachers discuss as a whole class what each group is doing, modelling for others the development of thought and action, research, refinement and debate which group attends such activities. These discussions may lead children to work in the 'atelier'. The atelier is a workshop, containing equipment and materials for making things, devoted to the graphic and plastic arts. It is separate from the classrooms and contains a huge range of resources for drawing and painting, work with light, clay, found materials and natural objects. It is a specialist room with a specialist teacher, trained as an artist, available to support to the children's work. The teacher/artist helps the children with techniques, research into forms and the production of items from their original ideas which they cannot yet, for reasons of safety or skill, undertake for themselves. In each classroom there are mini-ateliers where creative activities are planned and supported by the teachers.

At the end of the discussion session the children choose how they are going to spend the morning. Some will be invited by the teachers to join

*Independent Learning in the Foundation Stage*

adult-initiated activities, supported and observed by a teacher. Others will decide to work on their own projects in the atelier or the mini atelier. Further groups of children go off to play in the piazza area on construction, role-play, drawing or writing messages. A busy and purposeful hum of activity soon permeates the building, rising and falling with the rhythms of the children's work and interest.

This pre-school is not just open ended for free play. Some activities have been thoughtfully provided by the adults, following their observations during previous sessions, and the rooms have been carefully prepared and set before the children begin their work. Here is a typical collections of these 'enhanced activities':

**Clay in the mini-atelier.** Following observations, the teachers have noticed the children's interest in connecting diagonals, working on the flat surface of the table. The teachers want to pursue this theme, so they work with a group of children in this way, focusing on connections between diagonal lines of clay on the table.

**Message table in the classroom.** This table is set out with a wide range of different papers, pens, small pictures, photocopies of children's and adult's names, glue sticks, highlighters, collage bits (feathers, sequins, beads, etc.), envelopes and reduced photocopies of their own and others' pictures. In each classroom, there are individual letterboxes for each child, and many children send and receive letters every day.

**Exploring joining and folding.** Linking with the joining theme of the clay work, on one table there are strips of paper and staplers. The teacher has folded some pieces into zigzags. Otherwise, the children are free to explore the materials as they wish.

**Exploring colour and scent.** On another table is a selection of green and yellow papers, with green and yellow pens and inks. A vase of scented plants and leaves has also been placed on the table. It is suggested to the children that they might 'draw the scent'.

**Exploring light.** In a box near the overhead projector is a collection of transparent and translucent objects, all green and yellow. Some are recycled materials, others household objects such as bowls and funnels.

In the Atelier there are natural objects, flowers, fruit, cones and pieces of wood, books, photos and pictures to delight the eye and inspire creativity. In all the rooms there are games and puzzles, construction materials and bricks, resources for domestic role-play, cars and a range of other equipment on open-access shelving. The teachers in each room talk about activities

offered elsewhere in the school, in the piazza and in other classrooms (music and sound, mirrors, books, etc.). There is also discussion of the current projects under way in other classes, which children may join – or simply observe – if they want to. All activities are offered to all children, although some may be specifically offered to individuals or groups the teachers wish to observe or talk with. Children are free to join and leave activities as and when they wish. They are free to visit any part of the building.

All the children leave the group session having decided what they are going to do and where they will go. They work alone or in small groups, sometimes with an adult or fetching an adult to help if they need them. During this session all the children are inside the building; the space in the building makes movement easy and no area seems overcrowded, despite the number of activities going on.

At the end of the session (around 11:00am) the children gather in a large group. On most days they spend a short recreation period in the garden before lunch at 11:30. Lunch is an important part of the day; children carefully lay the tables with tablecloths and flowers. Teachers join the children for a leisurely lunch, during which there is time for conversation and enough quiet for relaxation. Lunch is followed by a further free play session and a siesta. Children are collected from 4:00, when they are all awake and quietly playing or talking. Some may stay at school until 7:30 if a special arrangement has been agreed.

This brief account fails to do justice to the sense of purpose apparent in all the children, their drive, their enthusiasm, their ideas and creativity.

## What are the special features that make the Reggio schools so successful?

| The practice | How this supports independence and autonomy |
| --- | --- |
| *The place and its people*<br>A factor in the success of the schools is the place and its people. Reggio is quite a small community, with a strong sense of identity. More important, however, is that the people of the city feel ownership of the schools – they built them (in some cases with their own hands), developed them and believe in what they stand for. There is a real commitment by families and the community, including politicians, to the schools and to children. There is community support for and pride in the achievements of the children. For example, the city | Children and teachers feel confident that the people they know value them and what they do. This results in high self-esteem.<br><br><br><br>Parents are true partners. |

tourist brochure has words and pictures by children, the theatre stage curtain was designed by children. Parents and members of the community are involved in projects and visits, sharing their working expertise with the children, taking them seriously. The children 'inhabit' the city and the community, bringing it into their learning. And there is a national tradition of valuing talk, discussion, debate, and in particular the graphic and figurative arts. These are central to the work of the schools.

Learning is set in a real-life context, encouraging the development of life skills and enabling all to see the relevance of what happens within the school to the life outside it.

*The schools and the system*
The group of schools is a manageable size. The teachers know each other and meet regularly during the year. The schools have developed together a shared set of principles, clear values, agreed outcomes and ways of working. This means that although each school has its own 'signature' and its own identity, they are very evidently part of the same system. There is a common structure to the day for all centres and schools. The staffing and organisation is common. Features of the architecture (the central piazza, the atelier or workshop, the message boxes), the projects, the place of mealtime and naps all appear in all schools. Schools and infant–toddler centres emphasise the superiority for children of experiences over methodologies. They say it is 'invented new, not handed down.'

Teachers have confidence in the system and feel ownership of it. This encourages an outstanding commitment to their work and how they approach it.

There is security in known systems, familiar patterns of organisation and a safe environment. This encourages both the teachers and the children to have the confidence to take risks.

Staff and parents work very hard. They have a commitment to 'struggle for the best' for their children. Staff remain in the schools for a long time, working with the same co-teacher for many years and developing shared expertise. There is a wholehearted commitment to the part creativity plays in learning, and an emphasis on talking, listening, play, making and thinking. There is also a commitment to process, not product, in children's learning. What is important is not the result, but how the children produced it. Staff and children are prepared to take risks in thought, discussion and in learning, because they have confidence in the support they have from other children, teachers and parents. Staff value the children's work – their words, thoughts, actions and artefacts. Their work is displayed with care and respect, often with transcripts of the children's words and thoughts. As a result children see their own and each other's efforts as important, and value them.

A minority of time is spent on the formal part of the curriculum

The formal part of the curriculum (i.e. that which is planned and guided by the teachers), at around 2.5 hours a day, is short compared with practice in the UK.

### The environment for learning

Although the schools and centres are not all in purpose-built premises, they have been skilfully and thoughtfully adapted to the children. They all have a spacious feel and plenty of light, with muted colours on walls and paintwork. Colour is provided by the children and their work. Storage is good, and areas are clearly delineated, while having an overall sense of openness. The atelier and the mini ateliers in each classroom provide access to a very wide range of accessible and well-presented resources, including recycled and found materials, tools and equipment. Message tables and message boxes for each child are a feature of all schools, and displays of natural objects (flowers, bark, shells, leaves, fruit) complement the children's work. There is plenty of room for unfinished work to be left out, and completed artefacts in all types of materials and media are displayed on the floor, on steps, shelves and tables, where they are handled and discussed. They are treated with care and respect by other children.

There is room for role play in the central piazza and in classrooms. Construction with bricks and blocks is given substantial space. Clay and other malleable materials are offered frequently. Activities such as these are available in both child and adult-initiated contexts.

The outside spaces are gardens, with trees, flowers, fruit, grass and hard surfaces. There is provision outside for sand and water play and there are tracks for cars and wheeled toys. The outside area is mostly used for recreation.

Displays reflect the respect everyone has for the words and work of the children.

Access to equipment and the availability of space and time all contribute to the children's involvement in their own learning.

Resources are of the highest quality and are well displayed, so that children can get at them easily.

Writing activities are not empty exercises. They have a purpose, meaning and individuality. Every message is valued on its own merits.

There is a good balance of child-initiated and teacher-initiated activities.

Children have ownership of their learning.

### The pace of the day and the projects

There is time during the day to talk at length, to play, to work, eat and sleep. There is enough space, so children are not overcrowded indoors or outdoors and enjoy a real sense of ownership of the environment. Mealtimes and rests have their proper place in the day. There is a clear programme and a timetable, but events flow in and out of each other without over organisation by adults or undue interruption of children's activities. When children arrive at school, there is time for free play and discussion with friends and teachers. Before they leave there is time to rest and reflect at the end of the day, and to talk about tomorrow.

There is a clear and consistent framework for the day and the use of spaces, but children own the activities which go on inside this framework. They are given time to discuss and plan what they will do.

### Relationships

There is stability for staff and children. The teachers and other staff stay for long periods with one class. Children enter a class and stay with this group and their two teachers for the whole of their time in the school. When they move from room to room as they get older they

Stability of staffing supports independence and confidence.

*Independent Learning in the Foundation Stage*

stay with their group and their teachers. This means that the teachers know the children and their families extremely well, and the routines and relationships are stable. Time is not wasted getting to know each other at the beginning of each year. There is frequent contact with parents on an informal and more formal basis. There is no headteacher and there are no office staff, so there is no barrier between the children, their parents and their teachers.

Teachers and children know each other well.

The work of the group and the individuals within it is regularly discussed at parents' meetings. On these occasions parents have the opportunity to look at, handle and discuss in detail the work of their children. Children's work is not sent home but is kept in the school, revisited and revised during projects, displayed (sometimes for quite long periods) and finally archived.

Children's work is treated as documentation of their learning. Nothing is discarded. It is kept and referred to later, becoming a celebration of achievement and a resource for future topics.

The teachers' pairings last many years, so that teachers know and support each other.

*The role of the teacher*
There is a wholehearted commitment to co-teaching. Teachers work in pairs, both having equal status and equal work. They also work with a 'pedagogista' - a consultant teacher employed across several schools, who gives guidance, discusses plans, offers observations and spends time in each of the schools during the day. The teachers from different schools meet each other at regular training sessions and meetings to compare notes and discuss their work. There is a clear but flexible planning framework based on agreed guidance.

Observation is a vital part of the teacher's job.

Teachers spend part of every day observing, listening to children and discussing their work and ideas with them. They use these observations to plan future activities and suggestions. They also reflect children's observations and comments back to them during subsequent discussions, helping them to develop their ideas and clarify their thinking. There is an obvious respect and value for children's work, thoughts and words.

The job of a teacher is valued and given time.

Discussion and observation are seen as an essential part of the work.

Observations are fed back to colleagues, parents and the children.

Each teacher has six hours each week of paid time to discuss their work, meet other teachers and the pedagogista, meet parents, revisit and share observations of children, and plan future activities. They also discuss common threads of child development, charting, for instance, how children's work with clay develops and how teachers can support that development. There is a strong commitment to their way of working. Teachers refer to themselves as 'researchers', working in the 'laboratory of the school', all the time discovering more about how children learn. The relatively short, formal, planned curriculum means that teachers must work with concentration during this time in order to observe and support progression in the ongoing projects.

Teachers have time to develop their knowledge of the theory and practice of education. Keeping up-to-date with recent research on learning is seen as an important part of their job.

The Reggio model has received worldwide attention and acclaim. Teachers elsewhere often envy the way things are arranged in the Reggio schools. All that space! Six hours paid time for planning and meetings! Such levels of parental commitment and involvement! Such support from politicians! However, if we want to adopt some of the Reggio methods in our own countries there are some factors that we would be wise to consider.

> It is a mistake to take any approach and assume like a flower you can take it from one soil and put it in another one. That never works. We have to figure out what aspects are most important to us and what kind of soil we need to make those aspects grow.
>
> *Howard Gardner, The Unschooled Mind; Basic Books (New edition) 2011*

Firstly, the wholesale transplanting of anything carries risks. The English, the Irish, the Scottish and the Welsh are very different from the Italians. Although British and Italian parents want the same things for their children, the parents in Reggio have a different culture, different history, different values and a different view of childhood.

Secondly, the Reggio schools have invented their own system. It has taken them many years and much hard work to develop. It has been influenced by of the methodologies and educational thinkers mentioned elsewhere in this book. If we borrow someone else's system we must take time to make it our own, to set it in our own context with our own families and children, our own political, social, economic and meteorological climate. We must be prepared to lobby our local and national politicians, we must convince the parents and others in the education system of the value of what we are doing. We must be prepared to work, to try things, to manage the failures as well as the successes, and to ensure that we are the best possible teachers. Only the best is good enough for Reggio schools – only the best should be good enough for our own children.

Above all, we must not forget the many excellent things we are already doing, and that the climate for change we are currently experiencing brings many opportunities.

Having issued all these caveats, here are some things which we think can – and should – be learnt from the Reggio teachers and children. They are things which will change our settings and give our children more opportunities to become those independent, autonomous learners we all seek.

- **Value the processes of play, talking, thinking**. Resist the pressure to focus all the time on outcomes rather than processes.
- **Value and expand creativity**. Release the creative energy in the children. Build in flexibility in work and planning. Challenge children to

do something large or complicated, something which will stretch them. Brainstorm with them and use what emerges to start a project.

- **Provide the best resources** you can afford, find, beg or borrow. Present them with care and improve access and variety.
- **Look at spaces**. Bring in the light; open the doors. Remember, the environment is the third teacher.
- **Give children time**. Don't rush them. The Reggio day has a lot of space for thinking and reflecting. Good thinking takes time!
- Remember that **observation involves listening as well as watching**. So watch, listen, notice, and act on what you see and hear. Time spent in observation is never wasted. Use what you observe to make yourself think, and to affect what you offer next. Document some of what you notice, and share it with others.
- **Record and display children's thoughts and words**. Enhance the displays of children's work by writing down what they say and think about their learning. Deliberately and overtly show that you value their work (not the same as bland approval of everything they do!).
- **Do what you know is right for you and the children**. Use your professional judgement, take some risks, follow the children.
- **Resist the pressures from above**, and the pressure to read and write too early. Recognise drawing as communication
- **Follow the recent guidance for the early years**. It will give you the permission to do what you know is right!
- **Keep children's work for longer**. Refer to it as the children develop their ideas. Encourage children to return to and rework things.
- **Promote parent partnership**. Commit yourself to real partnership in children's learning.
- **Value yourselves as practitioners**. Identify and be proud of what you already do well. Hold on to the joy of working with children.

## The High/Scope approach to early learning

Our second example of excellence was established in America, but as with Reggio philosophy, High/Scope features all over the world in a diverse range of settings, so many early years practitioners are familiar with the name. Having said this, they may not necessarily know what exactly the High/Scope approach involves.

High/Scope has its roots as far back as 1962 when David P Weikart, director of special services for the schools in Ypsilanti, Michigan, initiated the Perry Preschool Project, later known as the High/Scope Perry Preschool

Project. The project was specifically designed to respond to, and hopefully improve the chances of children Ypsilanti's poorest neighbourhoods who were persistently failing to get good grades in high school. These were children considered to be at risk; children who, over the years, had consistently scored low marks in intelligence and academic tests. Weikart's quest, and one that has been his lifelong consuming passion, was to reverse this trend through a search for 'causes and cures'. He was convinced that these students performed badly not because of a lack of innate intelligence, but because they had not had enough of the right sort of experiences before starting school. More recent research into the effects of early stimulation on brain development would certainly support his hypothesis.

> Looking at High/Scope research outcomes, the best appraisal of why the High/Scope Pre-school Curriculum works is this: The growth of children's initiative and positive social disposition in an active learning, early childhood setting can positively affect pre-schoolers' subsequent development and adult performance.
>
> *Hohman & Weikart, Educating Young Children; Active Learning Practices for pre-school and child care programmes; High/Scope Press; 2002*

After much consideration an ad hoc committee, comprising Weikart and three elementary school principals, was formed to explore what might be done to help these failing students. The committee held a series of discussions through which they examined such things as teaching methods, achievement and referrals to outside agencies. They explored ways in which the current patterns of failure could be counteracted. While they were engaged in this process the US Special Services Committee began to consider early intervention for three and four year olds, and Weikart was given permission to operate Michigan's first funded pre-school education programme.

Once the buildings had been found and the staff appointed, Weikart and the committee set themselves the task of designing a curriculum. They felt that if it was to support children's future academic growth and help them to break out of their cycle of underachievement, the curriculum would need to be cognitively orientated. They agreed on three basic criteria for curriculum development:

1. The curriculum should be underpinned by a coherent theory about teaching and learning.
2. Curriculum theory and practice must support each child's capacity to develop individual talents and abilities through ongoing opportunities for active learning.
3. All involved in the project should work as partners in all aspects of curriculum development to ensure that theory and practice received equal consideration.

Because there was no such approach in existence the Special Services Committee consulted a team of 'experts', who unfortunately advised against the project on the grounds that three and four year olds lacked the capacity to cope with such a curriculum! Undeterred, Weikart modified his plans and set up a carefully designed research project to compare the progress of the children in the pre-school programme with that of children without any pre-school programme experience. It was the work of Piaget that formed the basis for the first classroom programmes for three and four year olds, although over time there were disagreements about how Piaget's theories should best be applied in practice.

> ...knowledge arises neither from objects nor the child, but from interactions between the child and those objects.
>
> *Jean Piaget; The Language and Thought of the Child; Routledge; 2001*

This resulted in a research study of Piaget's work to see how theory and practice could be integrated in a daily classroom programme, and by degrees the High/Scope Curriculum was developed, with the plan-do-review method central to the whole approach.

Another key aspect of the programme was the involvement of parents and carers. Teachers worked to engage parents in thinking about the process of educating their children. Through discussion parents communicated to teachers the interests and needs of the children and their families, and teachers shared with parents information about child development and their methodology.

In 1967 Weikart launched a further research project, The High/Scope Pre-school Curriculum Comparison Project, designed to examine the effectiveness of three diverse pre-school curriculum models. It is this study that formed the basis for the longitudinal research that has shaped so much of our thinking about the impact of early years programmes on later achievement. The study's cumulative findings and most recent conclusions are reported in Schweinhart & Weikart, Lifetime Effects: The High/Scope Perry Preschool Study Through Age 40; High/Scope Press; 2005

This internationally recognised research shows massively powerful results and has influenced recent developments in early years education and care both here in the UK and abroad. It showed that by using the life

> In the High/Scope approach to early childhood education, adults and children share control. We recognise that the power to learn resides in the child, hence the focus on active learning practices. When we accept that learning comes from within, we achieve a critical balance in educating young children.
>
> The adult's role is to support and guide young children through their active learning adventures and experiences. I believe this is what makes our program work so well.
>
> *David P Weikart in Educating Young Children; Active Learning Practices for pre-school and child care programmes; High/Scope Press; 2002*

skills and positive attitudes promoted by the High/Scope programme, these children were actually able to break out of a cycle of deprivation. Attitudes acquired during these vital early years were sustained and paid dividends in later life.

Such evidence has huge implications for what happens to people in their earliest years, and not just for children who are considered to be 'at risk'. It is true that such an approach will probably have its most dramatic effects on those suffering from social and economic deprivation, but it will benefit any child because of the way it focuses on the strengths of the individual and promotes self-belief and empowerment. As children work within a High/Scope programme they learn crucial thinking skills, initiate and carry out their own learning activities and make independent decisions. The ability to do these things will benefit any child regardless of socio-economic background.

The High/Scope Curriculum has been continuously evolving since 1962 but its central principles have remained constant. At the heart of any High/Scope setting you will find active learning, because the approach is founded in the strong belief that young children learn best by being doing things themselves, and by being active in a stimulating environment, helped by adults who know and understand how to support and progress this way of learning. Children are not allowed to run riot; the emphasis is on shared control in a climate where children learn about relationships and develop their confidence and personal initiative.

The principles which guide the work of High/Scope practitioners in whatever context are:

- supporting active learning.
- observing and planning, using the High/Scope Key Experiences.
- engaging in positive adult-child interaction.
- arranging, equipping and supporting a dynamic learning environment.
- maintaining a consistent daily routine.
- observing and recording children's learning.
- involving families.
- working in teams to promote active learning.

The key elements are active learning, adult-child interaction, the learning environment, the daily routine and the plan-do-review process.

## Active learning

There are very few people working within early years who would not agree with the basic premise that young children learn best when they learn

*Independent Learning in the Foundation Stage*

actively. This requires that they have direct and immediate experience of objects, people, ideas and events and the opportunity and support to derive meaning from these experiences through reflection.

> A High/Scope training participant talks about the High/Scope difference: "I can understand why the 40-year study revealed the long-term impact of High/Scope with children at risk. High/Scope is ... about teaching children to initiate, discover, experience, and learn about ideas, events, and people; it is about children creating, experimenting, problem-solving, and resolving conflicts as they learn. High/Scope builds children up and changes lives." *Alice Escobar, Dallas, Texas (quoted on the High/Scope website)*

Through the exercise of personal initiative children explore, ask questions, solve problems and search for answers. They set their own goals and learn to cope with making mistakes. En route to achieving their goals they generate and try out strategies. Active learning has its foundations in 'doing'. It involves handling, changing things, moving, making things – not just looking. Action is climbing, pretending, modelling, discovering and comparing. It is about touching, tasting, feeling and exploring, all by yourself.

There are four critical elements of active learning:

- direct action on objects
- reflection on actions
- intrinsic motivation, invention and generativity
- problem solving

An active learning environment should provide daily opportunities for children to engage in these processes.

## Adult-child interaction

Meaningful active learning must be facilitated by high quality adult-child interaction, and practitioners in High/Scope settings spend time practising and developing positive interaction strategies. Much thought must be given to the ways in which young children think and learn, and support for active learning must be firmly embedded within the central principles of the approach. This involves adults in focusing on children's strengths, forming authentic relationships with children and adopting a problem-solving approach to social conflict. Great emphasis is also placed on the use of encouragement strategies, rather than a child management system based on praise and reward or blame and punishment.

The quality of the personal, social and emotional education is of great importance and high priority is given to the child's emotional wellbeing.

'Oh no', she says to me, 'you don't understand. X isn't naughty, they just can't always sort themselves out.'                                 *A parent*

'Even at home, if his sister is playing him up, he'll sit down and sort things out with her.'   *A parent*

Throughout the daily routine the adult is seen as the instigator of learning situations which will give children the opportunity to solve problems. The adult must constantly ask the question 'How can the teaching staff provide the key experiences most supportive of learning and development for each child, while acknowledging the child's own interests?'

What makes this interaction of such high quality is that adults feel able to risk sharing control with the children. This means that for much of their time children are empowered to be in charge of their own activities. It does not mean that adults withdraw and leave the children to get on with it alone. There is real commitment to supporting children; to starting with their interests and motivations, and allowing them to explore and experiment at their own level of knowledge.

High/Scope strives for a style of interaction that enables children to express their ideas, thoughts and feelings openly and coherently. It is children who decide the direction and content of their work and conversation. Working in partnership with the adults in their setting in a climate of shared control, children gain confidence in their ability as learners. (You can read more about the quality of adult-child interaction in Chapter 5).

## The learning environment

As in the Reggio Emilia model, the environment plays a crucial part in supporting children's active learning and problem solving, so organising and managing the learning environment is a very important part of the work of a High/Scope practitioner.

> In High/Scope centres and classrooms, children are active agents who construct their own knowledge of the world as they transform their ideas and interactions into logical and intuitive sequences of thought and action, work with diverse materials to create personally meaningful experiences and outcomes, and talk about their experiences in their own words.
>
> *High/Scope Institute; www,high/scope.org*

The adult must provide a rich array of developmentally appropriate materials and activities from which the children are invited to select, and it is not possible for children to do this without things being well organised and accessible. Children cannot plan what they want to do unless they are aware of the possibilities, so the working areas are zoned, with each area clearly labelled. The containers for the resources and materials are also carefully

*Independent Learning in the Foundation Stage*

organised and identified so that children can take responsibility for getting things out and putting them away again. In a good High/Scope setting there will be 'a place for everything and everything in its place'. Putting children in control demands a great deal of hard work and organisation.

Much thought is given to the nature of the resources and materials and care is taken to include a high proportion of open-ended and 'free and found' materials, designed to promote thinking skills, problem solving and representational development. Children have free access to the materials and are supported in choosing and deciding, setting goals, making plans and following them through.

We refer you to our discussion of a high quality learning environment in Chapter 6.

## The daily routine

A consistent daily routine is a key element of a High/Scope setting, where aspects of the day are arranged to best suit the needs of children, families and practitioners. This means that every day when the children arrive at the setting they know what to expect. They will also know that if there are to be any changes to the routine they will be told at the beginning of the session. This not only makes the children feel secure, vital given the emotional backgrounds and experiences of some of them, but also gives them a meaningful way of making sense of time. They can anticipate what will happen next, and this supports their active learning and gives them a high level of control over what they do during each part of the day.

Through a consistent daily routine, children have opportunities to work in a variety of groupings, through which they can engage in active learning and build a sense of community. A daily routine constructed to achieve an appropriate balance between adult initiation and child initiation will include:

Welcome Time
Small Group Time
Outside Time
Snack Time
Planning Time
Work Time
Review Time
Circle Time (large group time)

Compared to other preschool programs, preschool programs using the High/Scope model significantly contribute to the overall development of children from families of both low and middle socioeconomic status, particularly to the development of their initiative, social relations, and music and movement abilities. Use of the model helps improve the intellectual and social abilities of middle-class children with and without disabilities.

*Validity of the High/scope preschool Education Model 1; Lawrence J. Schweinhart; High/Scope; 2003*

*Identifying excellence* : 175

The parts of the day can be ordered to suit individual settings, although for obvious reasons the plan-do-review process must follow that order. This is the period of the day when children express their intentions, carry them out and reflect upon what they have done. Small Group Time is important because it allows the adults to introduce the children to new materials or reintroduce familiar ones. The things they select will be based on their observations of children's interests, key experiences and local events. Large Group Time allows for adults and children to initiate music and movement activities, re-enact stories and share play experiences and projects.

## The key experiences

For three to five year olds the High/Scope curriculum identifies ten areas of learning:

- language and literacy
- initiative and social relations
- movement
- music
- classification

- seriation
- number
- space
- time

Within these categories 66 'key learning experiences' have been identified. Working with the key experiences takes time and commitment, but it is the means by which adults discover a great deal about how three to five year-old children learn and think. It is also very rewarding for the practitioners. As they make anecdotal observations of the children engaging with these experiences, the observations can form the basis for planning and evaluating.

## Plan-do-review

Plan-do-review takes place daily in High/Scope settings and is central to the whole approach. It involves the adults in asking children to plan explicitly what they are going to do. They then begin to set goals for themselves and are supported in generating and evaluating alternative solutions to problems as a means to achieve their goals.

In daily adult planning sessions, for example, the question 'What do we want to plan for Vanessa tomorrow?' is coupled with a discussion about what Vanessa was involved in today.
*Educating Young Children; Active Learning Practices for pre-school and child care programmes; Mary Hohmann and David Weikart; High/Scope Press; 2002*

As they gain expertise in managing this process, children are acquiring massively important life skills. Learning to set goals, work towards them and deal with the setbacks that occur on the way is a hugely valuable

learning experience, but this does not happen without effort. Planning is a developmental process. When a three year old enters a High/Scope setting he or she probably won't have the faintest idea what a plan is. They will learn this over time as they experience the planning process embedded in the real-life, active learning provided in the setting.

Initially a child's choices and decisions will be expressed non-verbally through pointing, and simply selecting those materials and resources that are of the greatest interest, but as time goes on they will begin to engage in the processes of choosing and deciding with ever-increasing complexity and sophistication. Through planning, children learn to create and express their intentions, both individually and in groups, and they experience the joys and frustrations of working towards and achieving a goal. In settings where practitioners are very experienced, children are enabled to see that there is no such thing as failure; there are only outcomes – and if we are not happy with the outcome we achieve, we change our actions to get a different outcome.

Work time involves the children in carrying out their plans. It provides adequate time for trial and error, time to generate new ideas, practise and keep going until they succeed. Throughout this time the children exercise a high degree of personal independence. Adults respect their need to explore, and understand what can be gained when self-motivated children engage in active learning.

Review time is for children to reflect upon their experiences in a wide variety of ways. Practitioners use a range of planning and recall strategies designed to maintain children's interest and motivation, and it does not take long for the children to become adept at the process. As they gain experience and confidence they plan and review with increasing logic, verbal ability and skill. Through engaging in this process children experience both immediate and long-term benefit.

## Conclusion

High/Scope is an approach to early years education that has been demonstrated by careful studies over a long period to offer benefits to children, families, practitioners and society in general. It is only one of a number of models of early years practice, but it is a model that, well implemented, can provide excellence.

In the words of Serena Johnson, Director of High/Scope UK between 1995 and 2000:

> Children, families, practitioners and society generally benefit from the approach. Families and practitioners benefit because High/Scope provides practitioners with a stimulating and rewarding method of working, encourages managers to

place more value in training and encourages parents and practitioners to extend their expectations for children and themselves. Children and society benefit ... because (High/Scope) provides a learning approach which meets the developmental and cultural needs of children and also meets the demands of our fast-changing, technological society.

It provides a 'competency based' curriculum at a time when, as we know from research on the brain, children's learning potential is at its greatest. It can work in harmony with the curriculum laid down by government while recognising the needs of each child to have an 'individual learning plan' and the competencies of 'learnacy', citizenship, relating to people, managing situations and information, thus enhancing opportunities to become, in the long-term, fulfilled adults and contributors to society.

For those who want to know more about High/Scope, and particularly about how the model may be applied in a British setting, publications and other information are available from the UK High/Scope site – www.high-scope.org.uk

Readers may also wish to extend their reading by investigating other new initiatives, such as Te Whaariki in New Zealand or the Forest School approach developed in Scandinavia.

The case studies describing Reggio Emilia Schools and High/Scope systems are not intended to provide universal solutions. We have included them because they offer clear examples of the principles we are advocating applied consistently and successfully over a long period.

Early childhood education has enormous individual, social and economic benefits. For example, early childhood programmes complement the roles of parents and other carers in raising children during the early years. The early childhood years set the foundation for life, ensuring that children have positive experiences and that their needs for health, stimulation and support are met, and that they learn to interact with their surroundings.

*Early Childhood Education: A Global Scenario; A study conducted by the Education International ECE Task Force; June 2010 www.ei-ie.org*

The sort of longitudinal studies relating to High/Scope do not, as far as we know, exist for the Reggio schools, but their track record is demonstrable in a different way, through the achievements of Reggio children and the culture and dynamics of the city. There are also many books available which describe the practice in Italy and throughout the world, where the same approaches have been adopted. We hope you will gain inspiration, ideas and enthusiasm from these dedicated pioneers – as we did. However, it is important to remember that in all countries and all settings it is the impact of the adults – teachers, practitioners, carers, assistants, helpers – that will most affect the experiences of the children and the outcomes of their learning.

# Chapter 18:
# Managing change

If the principles of independent learning are important to you and if you want to promote them in your setting, their implementation, support and evaluation will need careful management. Everyone associated with the setting – staff, children, parents, governors and management groups, local advisers – has to be clear about what you intend, why you believe change is needed, and what their part will be in ensuring success. Judgements of quality should not be left solely to inspectors. Practitioners should know their own setting and have a good idea of the levels of quality in their provision long before an inspection team crosses the threshold.

This chapter assumes you wish to promote independence and autonomy for the children in your setting, and addresses the tasks of managing the initiatives and processes to get you there. It makes recommendations covering the way you declare your intentions, promote teamwork, manage whole setting issues, describe and promote aims and principles, train staff, change practice and involve the children and their parents. If your personal response to this book has been positive and if you feel that you want to use what you have read to identify existing good practice in your setting and to develop that quality further, this chapter will give you some starting points.

There are six sections:

> Every child deserves the best possible start in life and support to fulfil their potential. A child's experience in the early years has a major impact on their future life chances. A secure, safe and happy childhood is important in its own right, and it provides the foundation for children to make the most of their abilities and talents as they grow up. When parents choose to use early years services they want to know that provision will keep their children safe and help them to thrive.
>
> *EYFS Statutory Framework; DCSF; May 2008*

1. Auditing present provision
2. Coming to a shared view, and declaring intentions
3. Keeping everyone informed and involved
4. Planning for action
5. Observing and monitoring progress
6. Identifying successes and areas for further improvement

The Guidance for the EYFS says: These principles require practitioners to plan a learning environment, indoors and outdoors, that encourages a positive attitude to learning through rich and stimulating experiences and by ensuring that each child feels included. This is demonstrated when practitioners:

- encourage children to make choices and develop independence by having equipment and materials readily available and well organised.
- provide resources that inspire children and encourage them to initiate their own learning.
- give the children the space they need for their activities.

This statement, together with others within the EYFS Guidance, gives a clear lead to our practice and to the evaluation of quality in our provision. How can we know if we are achieving this high quality?

The indicator given by OFSTED for 'outstanding performance in achievement in the EYFS' is:

All children make significant gains in their learning and have consistently good and often excellent levels of achievement in relation to their starting points and capabilities. Children play a dynamic role in their learning. They offer their ideas and respond to challenges with great enthusiasm. They show exceptionally high levels of independence, curiosity, imagination and concentration. They use all their senses to actively explore and solve problems.

*Inspecting the Early Years Foundation Stage; Guidance for Inspectors; OFSTED; 2009*

We will keep this guidance associated criteria in mind as we explore what is involved in managing and guaranteeing quality provision.

# 1. Auditing present provision – why is this important?

It is easy (and dangerous) to assume that there is no existing good practice in your setting, that there are no successes, that changes and improvements start at zero. This is rarely, if ever, true. However much we want things to be better, if we look positively and realistically at present practice we can all find some foundations on which developments can be built. There is nothing more demoralising than to be told that nothing is being done, everything must change, we must start again at the beginning.

The first step is to look positively at your setting, identifying existing strengths as well as improvements for the future. By using some of the questions in this book it is possible to construct a short audit or discussion document which will help you with this evaluation.

*Independent Learning in the Foundation Stage*

## 2. Coming to a shared view and declaring intentions - why is this important?

If you don't come to a shared view on independence and independent learning with colleagues and parents, you will at best decrease your effectiveness, and at worst children and adults will be confused by different messages from different people.

Ideally you and the parents and carers of the children will have a common view about independence, and this will have been arrived at through discussion and an honest exchange of views. These views will be clearly communicated when parents choose to send their children to your setting, and will be taken into account as you discuss their child's education and care. Remember that parents, too, are early years specialists but most are not acquainted with the detailed guidance offered to practitioners and inspectors, and therefore do not have the professional vocabulary for articulating aims and discussing children.

We recommend that in arriving at this shared view you concentrate on outcomes - how you want the children to be and what you want them to be able to do. You might find it helpful to look again at the definitions of independent learners and the descriptions of their capabilities in the middle sections of this book. They make a useful starting point for discussions with parents at meetings and through questionnaires. Your brochure or prospectus will augment these by giving a clear indication of how you work and the skills and attitudes you value.

Practitioners working in settings should have regular opportunities to discuss their views on the style as well as the content of the curriculum, coming to a shared understanding of the skills children will be developing and the ways in which adults support them through sensitive observation and interaction. Sections 2 and 3 of this book will help you to consider the role of the adults, the setting and the organisation of activities to enable children to become independent learners.

It will be important to communicate the outcomes of reviews and agreements. Your documentation should make reference to the principles contained in the official or local guidance, but you will probably want to flavour it with the essentials of your own discussions and state in writing the commitment of your setting to independent learning. Written statements not only help you clarify your own views, they communicate

A further challenge is 'the review, analysis and planning, with a group of colleagues, for further use of the information gained. This takes time, commitment and skill.'

*Louise Boyd Cadwell, Bringing Reggio Emilia Home; Teachers College Press; 1997*

to visitors such as inspectors and advisers, and provide a way into your own monitoring of your provision.

As you agree and construct statements about your curriculum, you will inevitably become aware of the links between elements of independent learning and other policy statements, particularly those dealing with equality of opportunity, special needs, cultural diversity and race relations. In school settings these statements will need to be checked to ensure that they are consistent with statements and policies in the school brochure, prospectus or handbook.

## 3. Keeping everyone informed and involved – why is this important?

The processes recommended above sometimes lead to arguments and conflicts of views, and it is as well to recognise this. There are still people around who think that young children need a formal curriculum and who see children's independence as a threat to the authority and role of the practitioners. However, if everyone is involved in discussions and decisions there is much more chance of a common intention and a common approach. Children, parents, management groups and practitioners all need to be involved at different levels and by a range of means. Meetings, discussions, questionnaires, newsletters and notices all have their place in ensuring that information is communicated and opinions are sought on current quality and future intentions.

The views of children are particularly important when developing independence. How can you develop yourself if you don't get a voice in your own learning?

## 4. Planning for action – why is this important?

One of the outcomes of your audit and reviewing processes will be suggestions and ideas of things you want to do and provide. Wish lists are by their nature long, and your list of improvements may seem very daunting – even more difficult to manage than the previous provision!

Get the list into some sort of order by constructing an action plan. This will establish priorities for action i.e. what to do first, next and last. This will help you put the changes you want to make in a programme for development, which can be costed and incorporated in the improvement or management plan for the setting. This reduces panic by making things more manageable and showing how changes can be implemented over time and within the budget.

*Independent Learning in the Foundation Stage*

You might consider adopting the following way of managing an action programme. Here are some of the areas you will probably want to address:

- Space, including improvements to the building (e.g. better access to the outside, redecoration, relocating display boards, smartening the entrance area)
- Storage (e.g. additional shelving, storage boxes and crates, replacing existing containers and boxes)
- Equipment (e.g. extending the choice of brush sizes, collage materials, outside play equipment)
- Organisation (e.g. longer access to the garden, flexible snack and drink times, circle time)
- Staffing and relevant qualifications and experience.
- Training and staff development needs (e.g. observation and intervention, understanding play, asking questions)
- Contacts with and involvement of children (e.g. discussions, observations, suggestions)
- Contacts with and involvement of parents (e.g. questionnaires, improved information, notice boards, photo books).

Your plan will need to take account of cost, urgency, importance and timescale. All these will vary.

The **cost** of implementation:
- Some suggestions will have high costs (such as altering the building to provide access to an inaccessible play area)
- Some suggestions will be cheap (such as removing the doors from cupboards, lowering the handles on doors)
- Some suggestions can be done at no cost except for the time taken (such as rearranging the furniture to improve access to an inaccessible play area).

The **timescale** for implementation:
- Some suggestions will take a long time to implement (such as raising the money to build a safety fence, or arranging training for the staff)
- Some suggestions take little or no time to implement (such as removing or reorganising furniture or involving the children in discussions).

The **urgency** of implementation:
- Some suggestions will be considered very urgent (particularly those associated with health and safety, or talking to parents about the changes you plan).
- Some will be less urgent, although desirable.

The **importance** of implementation:
- Some suggestions will be very important to you
- Some suggestions may be considered less important.

Sorting out these competing priorities can be tricky! One way to approach it is to construct a list like the one below, giving each action a priority rating from 1 (highest) to 5 under each of the above criteria. It is also helpful to make an estimate of cost, where you can. This will enable you to separate the urgent from the important and the essential from the desirable, as well as helping you see what can be afforded.

| Action | Cost | Time | Importance | Urgency |
|---|---|---|---|---|
| Move pinboards to child height | £15 (2) | 2 hrs | 4 | 4 |
| Remove wall between nursery & veranda | £500 (5) | 3 days | 4 | 3 |
| Replace broken stay on outside door | £5 | 2 hrs | 5 | 5 |
| Introduce flexible snack time | none | 1 day | 2 | 2 |

## 5. Observing and monitoring progress – why is this important?

We all know that it is possible to have wonderful paperwork, which looks very impressive but has no relation to the reality of children's experiences. In order to make sure that what we say is what we do, we must spend time looking at the practice and the experiences of children in our settings. Direct observation is the most effective way of evaluating the quality of what we do.

Observing practice helps us at each stage of development. If we observe before embarking on change, we get a baseline for development. If we observe during times of change we get a good idea of how the changes are progressing and of any emerging problems. If we observe after the major period of change, during the consolidation stage, we have the basis for evaluating the match with our original intentions and assessing the resulting improvements in provision.

There are three more common types of observation with varying degrees of formality. We will probably want to make use of them all, but to do this we need to be sure of the job of each and what it can and cannot offer.

*Independent Learning in the Foundation Stage*

1. We all make **casual, informal observations** all the time as we experience our setting. We collect first hand information by seeing, hearing, touching and even smelling the environment. We constantly make judgements as we encounter various pieces of evidence, and adjust our opinions of the quality of what we see as a result. These observations are subjective, usually without clear criteria, and are made very quickly, often while we are doing something else. They are very valuable, but they are 'scattergun' observations, often reflecting feelings rather than facts. The information we acquire in this way is usually verbal and anecdotal. We rarely write it down but nevertheless it is some of the most useful evaluation data available to us, an ongoing impression about what we have experienced.

   Professionals have become much more practised at giving feedback to colleagues resulting from formal or informal observations. Parents and other visitors may well be more reserved, preferring to share judgements with others outside the setting rather than telling us. You will be familiar with the parent who talks at the gate about what she saw, sometimes in her subjectivity missing the point of what is going on and the reasons for it – "'They can have their drink any time they like, I think they should make them all sit down together like they used to do. I don't know why they have changed.' This information is important (not least in this instance by telling us that we have not communicated effectively to this parent and possibly others), but we often have to work hard to get it and sometimes only acquire it through chance or hearsay.

2. **Structured observations** can be undertaken by anyone who has time, but are usually planned by practitioners. A structured observation needs clear and agreed criteria. These should be drawn from the documentation of the setting and few in number. Such observations give valuable feedback, enhanced by the practitioner's knowledge of the setting, child development and the intentions of the documentation. One member of staff may take a feature of recent development, for instance the use by children of newly organised collage materials. The practitioner will watch the children as they work in this area, making notes of exactly what happens. She may use a camera, video or tape recorder to help with the collection of evidence. This is then shared with the whole team, who are better able to judge the effectiveness of the changes they have made. Structured observations are a strong feature of all of the high quality practice we have seen.

3. **Tracking** individuals and groups is a method of observation which links well with your intended outcomes. If you have made a statement about the characteristics, behaviours and attitudes you hope will result from

more autonomy and independence, you may want to track a child over a period of time to see whether these characteristics and attitudes are in fact resulting from the strategies you have implemented. For instance, are children making independent choices? Are they more able to resolve conflict, delay gratification, work together on projects, sustain concentration? This information is not easily acquired from a single 20 minute observation. It takes a range of perspectives from different observers (including parents and children) gathered over a period of time in different places and through a variety of activities. Such 'deep' information is rich in content, and should give you food for thought. It is the best possible way to find out whether the changes you are making are having an effect.

Where possible, observations should involve all the stakeholders in the setting, not just management and practitioners. Children, parents, members of the community, schools and other settings to which the children transfer all have a contribution to make. The important thing to remember is that these inputs won't just happen on their own; they need a structure and procedures.

Practitioners will have the best opportunity and usually the most experience of observing during sessions. However, their opinion is coloured by knowledge of the setting and their objectivity may be compromised by their closeness. Parents and other adult visitors can be involved in direct observation or through questionnaires and interviews. When you construct your questionnaire or interview questions, make sure you have included all the things you want to know and that the questions are clear, free from unnecessary jargon, and easy to understand. Children, too, should contribute their observations and feelings to the debate about quality. They may not be able to carry out systematic observations or fill in questionnaires, but if invited and encouraged they can and will give their opinions in a range of ways. Drawing, puppets, small world, role play, taking photos and playing games can expand the more usual circle time and discussion opportunities. If you encourage children to talk about how they feel as well as describing what they do, they will be able to contribute a huge amount of valuable information to add to your observations.

## 6. Identifying successes and areas for further improvement – why is this important?

We often forget to recognise and celebrate the things that are going well. We sometimes overlook the achievements and concentrate on the things that

*Independent Learning in the Foundation Stage*

still need doing or are going less well. It gives everyone a good feeling to celebrate, and this doesn't mean forgetting the pointers to further improvement.

When you are collecting monitoring information, remember to record the good things. Don't ask people to identify only the things they don't like – ask them for the things they like and feel are successful. Small children are able to draw or choose pictures of things they enjoy doing or experiencing, things that make them happy, anxious, sad or scared. Parents sometimes feel that a consultation is an invitation to complain, so give them a structure which will make sure that they also identify successful features of the setting and positive effects on their children. Make a public display of your successes. Put up a notice on the parents' board, send a letter home, give yourselves a sticker. Have a party! Giving a high priority to your successes as well as to the things you want to improve helps you to move on to the next challenges with confidence.

Finally, we can think of no better advice to a management team considering implementing a new or revised programme than that given by an early years adviser in Effective Early Learning, who says:

> Be very clear about why you want to do it. Be convinced you are doing it for the benefit of the children first and foremost. If you are not, don't bother because you will never be focused in the way that you carry it forward because you won't know why you are doing it. And then go for it, be well organised, structure it so you can support your colleagues properly, recognise that they are going to have times of difficulty and be ready to cope with it when they need support. And manage it so that everyone feels they can play a part in shaping it.

**Here are some questions** that it may be helpful to consider when you review how you manage development and change in your setting.

- Do you have clear, shared, written statements setting out the way you work and the outcomes you intend? Are these tested in practice to confirm that what you say is what you do?
- Is observation an accepted feature of the way you work? Are practitioners in the habit of carrying out frequent, informal observations as well as contributing to the more formal structures?
- Do you collect information from parents on the aspects of the setting they like, and those they feel less sure or confused about?
- Do you have ways of involving children in talking about how they feel as well as what they have been doing?
- Do you work in a culture where successes and achievements are recognised and celebrated?

# The Last Word

We began this book with a statement about the importance of independent-minded and autonomous individuals to a free society, and by pointing out how attitudes and characteristics such as open mindedness, working with and caring for others, self control and self reliance, together with a constructive approach to problems, have their seeds in early childhood experiences.

The description of the EYFS and the establishment of the goals for early learning are huge and important steps. So is the emphasis on the pre-school years and the dawning realisation that both deprivations and enrichments in early life will have a profound effect on an individual later. However, there is further to go, because it is how these new initiatives and priorities are addressed in the huge variety of early years settings which will determine whether or not they are successful.

> Low expectations, based on the stereotypical view of children as being irrational, irresponsible and selfish may affect the opportunities we offer to children. As a result, children may not have the chance to show us how capable they are, or develop their capability to make decisions, take responsibility or care for others.
>
> *Judy Miller, Never Too Young;*
> *Save the Children; 2003*

We have tried to give some pointers to show how this might be done, and we did this in three stages. Firstly, we traced the emergence of modern views of child development and related these to advances in brain research and child psychology. We think this is important, because while skilful practice will always be at the heart of effective early years education, it is increasingly important for us to be able to justify what we are doing and relate it to the historical views and the theory of child development. Next we offered a definition and description of the independent learner, showing how the characteristics of independence emerge in young children and exploring the influence of adults and the physical environment. In the third stage we examined two highly effective approaches to early education, in Reggio Emilia and the High/Scope Programmes, and gave some pointers to managing some of the changes you may wish to implement as a result of reading this book.

Our aim has been to produce a book that will be of practical help to everyone engaged with or in early years settings. In the hurly burly of coping with every day it is easy to lose sight of key principles. However, there is one to which practitioners should cling at all costs. It is 'trust the children'. Most children are by their nature 'programmed' to learn. They want to find out about things, to explore and to discover. Often they have ideas about how to do this. If you allow them to, you will be surprised and delighted by where they will lead you and where, with your help and support, they are able to go. Trust them, listen to what they have to say, and do not be afraid to let them take control. Give them the benefit of your mature judgement without stifling their independence and creative spirit. These things are not easy, but they are improved by sensitivity and practice. And, thankfully, they are already present in many settings. We should like to record our thanks to and our appreciation of the many excellent practitioners we have met in this country and in other places, and whose work we have been privileged to see. We could not have written this book without the benefit of their wisdom and insight. We hope we have done justice to what we have learnt from them.

The last word? No, because that, as always, belongs to the children:

A girl (almost five) went in the morning to a setting where she was given a great deal of freedom to choose activities and get out her own equipment. In the afternoons she went to a different setting where everything was done for the children. She described the difference:

'If I could, I'd choose to stay here all day. All the people everywhere are nice, but here I plan my programme with Sally... she's my keyworker... and all the kids plan what they will do and then we can get it all by ourself. At first, I wasn't allowed at the other place and I never knew and I got told off for helping myself to the scissors. I remember crying ... now I know I'm not allowed. I don't know why.'

*Listening to Four Year Olds; Jacqui Cousins; NCB; 2003*

# Bibliography

**Abbott**, Lesley & **Nutbrown**, Cathy; Experiencing Reggio Emilia; Open University Press; 2001

**Bertram**, Tony, **Pascal**, Chris; Early Years Education: An International Perspective; Centre for Research in Early Childhood, Birmingham; QCDA/NFER; 2002 www.inca.org.uk

**Bowlby**, John; Childcare and The Growth of Love; Penguin; 1990

**Brosterman**, Norman; Inventing Kindergarten; Harry N Abrahams; 1997

**Cadwell**, Louise Boyd; Bringing Reggio Emilia Home; Teachers' College Press 1997

**Ceppi & Zini**; Children, Spaces, Relationships; Reggio Children 1999

**Clark and Moss**; Listening to Young Children, the Mosaic Approach; NCB; 2001

**Csikszentmihalyi**, Mihalyi; Flow: The Psychology of Happiness; Rider; 2002

**Donaldson**, Margaret; Children's Minds; HarperCollins; 1986

**Dryden**, Gordon and **Voss**, Jeannette; The Learning Revolution; Network Education Press; 2005

**Edwards, Gandini & Forman**, The 100 Languages of Children; Ablex Publishing Corporation; 1998

**Finch**, Sue; An Eye for an Eye Leaves Everyone Blind; Save the Children; 2003

**Fisher**, Robert; Teaching Children to Think; Nelson Thornes; 2005

**Gardner**, Howard, The Unschooled Mind; Basic Books; 1993

**Ginsberg and Opper**; Piaget's Theory of Intellectual Development; Prentice Hall; 1979

**Goleman**, Daniel; Emotional Intelligence; Bloomsbury; 1996

**Goldschmeid**, Eleanor & **Jackson**; Sonia, People Under Three; Routledge; 2003

**Gopnik**, Alison, **Meltzoff**, Andrew and **Kuhl**, Patricia; How Babies Think; Phoenix; 2001

**Greenland**, Penny; Hopping Home Backward; Jabadeo; 2000

**Greenman**, Jim; Caring Spaces, Learning Places: children's environments that work. 1988. Exchange Press

*Independent Learning in the Foundation Stage*

**Gussin Paley**, Vivian; In Mrs Tulley's Room (and other titles); Harvard University Press; 2003

**Handy**, Charles; The Empty Raincoat; Random House;1995

**Holt,** John; Learning All The Time; DeCapo Press; 1990

**Hohmann**, Mary and **Weikart**, David; Educating Young Children; Active Learning Practices for pre-school and child care programmes; High/Scope Press; 2002

**Isaacs**, Susan; The Educational Value of the Nursery School; 1954

**Lindon**, Jennie; Too Safe for Their Own Good?; NCB Publications 2003

**Louv**, Richard; Last Child in the Woods; Atlantic Books; 2010

**Meyer**, Bill; Haywood Naomi, Sachdev Darshan and Faraday Sally; What is independent learning and what are the benefits for pupils? (A literature review of Independent Learning Report 051; Department for Children, Schools and Families Research; 2008

**Medlicott**, Mary; Stories for young children and how to tell them; Featherstone; 2010

**Miller**, Judy; Never Too Young; Save the Children; 2003

**Nutbrown**, Cathy; Threads of Thinking; Sage; 2011

**Pascal**, C and **Bertram**; A D; Effective Early Learning: Case Studies of Improvement; Hodder and Stoughton; 1997

**Pagani**, Dr. Linda S; Quebec Longitudinal Study of Child Development; University of Montreal; 2010

**Piaget**, Jean; The Language and Thought of the Child; Routledge; 2001

Reggio Children; A Journey into the Rights of Children; Reggio Children; 1995

**Rose**, Colin and **Nicholl**; Accelerated Learning for the 21st Century; Piatkus Books; 1998

**Rosen**, Michael (Children's Laureat) in Every Child a Talker; DCSF; 2008

**Rousseau**, Jean Jacques, Emile; Phoenix; 1993

**Schweinhart**, Larry, & **Weikart**, David; Lifetime Effects: The High/Scope Perry Preschool Study Through Age 40; High/Scope Press; 2005

**Schweinhart**, Lawrence J.; Validity of the High/scope preschool Education Model 1; High/Scope; 2003

**Tsantis**, L; Creating the Future, Technology as the Catalyst; www.newhorizons.org

**Valentine**, Marianne; The Reggio Emilia Approach; Scottish Consultative Council on the Curriculum; 1999

**Vygotsky**, Lev, Thought and Language; MIT Press; 1998

**Weikart**, David P in Educating Young Children; Active Learning Practices for pre-school and child care programmes; High/Scope Press; 2002

## Government Guidance

**Framework for Children's Learning for 3 to 7-year-olds in Wales**; Department for Children, Education, Lifelong Learning and Skills; 2008

**Finding and Exploring Young Children's Fascinations**; DCSF; 2010

**EYFS** Statutory Framework; DCSF; May 2008

**EYFS** Practitioner Guidance; DCSF; May 2008

**EYFS Practitioner Guidance cards** 'The Learning Environment' 'Creative Development' 'Play and Exploration' 'Creativity and Critical Thinking' from the EYFS pack; DCSF; May 2008

**EYFS Effective practice guidance**: 'The Learning Environment' 'Messy Play' 'Creative and Critical Thinking'; EYFS pack, CD Rom; DCSF; 2008 Finding and Exploring Young Children's Fascinations; DCSF; 2010

**Inspecting the Early Years Foundation Stage**; Guidance for Inspectors; OFSTED; 2009

**Learning Playing and Interacting**; DCSF; 2009

**Mark Making Matters**; DCSF; 2008

**QCA, Curriculum Guidance for the Early Years Foundation Stage**; QCA; 2000

## Websites

**Reggio Children**; Zerosei; www.zerosei.comune.re.it

**High/Scope Institute**; www,high/scope.org